THE ECONOMIC CONSEQUENCES OF A NUCLEAR FREEZE

THE ECONOMIC CONSEQUENCES OF A NUCLEAR FREEZE

By William D. Hartung
with
Benjamin Goldman
Rosy Nimroody
Rochelle Tobias

Edited By
Alice Tepper Marlin
Paula Lippin

A COUNCIL ON ECONOMIC
PRIORITIES PUBLICATION

Managing Editor:
Neal Karrer

Design and Typesetting:
Fine Lines Graphic Services, Inc.

Cover:
Bill Smith

Statistical Typing
Bill Funk

International Standard Book Number: 0-87871-023-X
© 1984 by the Council on Economic Priorities
All rights reserved.

Council on Economic Priorities
84 Fifth Avenue, New York, N.Y. 10011
212/691-8550

Printed in the United States of America

Table of Contents

Acknowledgements

The Council was fortunate indeed to have the advice and comments of advisors who carefully reviewed our manuscript. Their comments enabled us to strengthen both our research and its presentation. Responsibility for the study, of course, rests solely with the Council on Economic Priorities. We thank the following advisors: Gene Carroll (Nuclear Weapons Freeze Campaign), Steve Daggett (Coalition for a New Foreign and Military Policy), Robert W. DeGrasse Jr. (Kennedy School of Government, Harvard), David Gold (Institute on the Military and the Economy), Mary Gardiner Jones (Consumer Interest Research Institute), Pam McIntyre (Nuclear Weapons Freeze Campaign National Clearinghouse), Carol O'Cleireacain (District Council 37, AFSCME), Lee B. Thomas, Jr. (Vermont American Corporation), Linda Shaw (Investor Responsibility Research Center), and Tom Webster (Center for the Biology of Natural Systems). There were others who served the same role but who prefer to remain anonymous.

All of us on the staff and the Board of the Council wish to thank the foundations and individuals whose generous donations enabled us to undertake this study: The Boehm Foundation, the Careth Foundation, Pat Hastings, the New Land Foundation, the North Shore Unitarian Veatch Program, George Wallerstein, and an anonymous donor. Generous general support grants from other foundations and individuals, including our trustees, enabled the Council the complete this enterprise. On the Council's 15th anniversary, we extend special thanks to the Marie C. and Joseph C. Wilson Foundation, the Scherman Foundation, the Stephen Memorial Fund, and the Rockefeller Family Fund for their extraordinary support.

Preface

An idea for change in the way our government works, one as fundamental as a proposed nuclear arms Freeze, is guaranteed to engender strong reaction in every sector of society, especially a society as pluralistic as the United States'.

We have seen the Freeze mature from such an idea, sounding nearly too simple to be valid, to a viable political alternative debated at every level of government from local school boards to the White House and the halls of Congress.

We have seen further the Freeze opponents search and grope for every available argument to oppose the Freeze to protect their own political, economic, or personal goals. One of the recurring themes is that military spending is "good" for the economy and the impact of a Freeze would be devastating.

The Council on Economic Priotities' record of accomplishment in research on the economic impact of military spending is impressive. They have published two highly respected works in two years: *The Costs and Consequences of Reagan's Military Buildup* and *Military Expansion, Economic Decline.*

This new volume, *The Economic Consequences of a Nuclear Freeze,* by William Hartung, is, in my view, the most substantial contribution to our understanding of how a Freeze will affect employment, budget savings, Federal deficits, and business development. It documents the opportunity costs of proceeding with the current nuclear weapons buildup.

My life is dedicated to the effort to stop and reverse the nuclear arms race before it literally ends the human race, so I welcome this objective study. Furthermore, as a manufacturer and corporate executive, I believe that the Council's tough-minded, conscientious research clearly outlines how crucial, and potentially beneficial, it is for corporate America to vigorously promote a bi-lateral Freeze on nuclear arms. Now is the time for us to cut our losses and shift to invest our wealth of resources in real rather than illusory national security.

The Economic Consequences of a Nuclear Freeze will help many people to understand the actual human and financial consequences of our participation in the nuclear arms race, and begin to envision a healthier, safer, and more viable future for America.

The greatest problems facing our country today—unemployment, budget deficits, on-again, off-again recessions—would look very different, and far more soluble, if a Freeze were implemented.

I've sought to encourage corporate participation in the Freeze debate, not only among those concerned about peace, but from all who understand the benefits of dismantling our military economy and converting it to a pro-people and pro-business one. This study can play a critical role in clarifying these arguments and helping further the cause of peace.

> —Harold Willens
> President and Chairman (Ret.)
> Factory Equipment Corp. and
> Wilshop Corp.
> Author of *The Trimtab Factor:*
> *How Business Executives Can*
> *Help Solve the Nuclear Weapons Crisis*

Introduction

The Freeze, the Economy, and Nuclear Arms Control

The development of new nuclear weapons systems has become a primary political issue in the United States over the past three years, rivaled in significance only by debates on how to revive the US economy. Proposals for curbing nuclear weapons production as well as insuring that these weapons are never used have proliferated in the executive branch, the Congress, and at state and local levels. The National Committee of the Nuclear Weapons Freeze Campaign requested that CEP examine an important dimension of the nuclear arms control debate: how would a halt in the production of new nuclear warheads and their delivery vehicles affect the US economy? That is how this study was conceived.

A bilateral US-USSR nuclear weapons Freeze differs from other current arms control initiatives—it envisions a prompt halt to *all* production of new nuclear missiles, bombers, and warheads. [1] Its economic ramifications, therefore, are much broader than those of other nuclear arms control proposals. For example, the Reagan Administration's Strategic Arms Reduction Talks (START) proposal calls for *continued* production of a new generation of nuclear weapons systems alongside the eventual dismantling of those currently deployed.

CEP's aim is to understand and quantify the economic effects of a halt in nuclear weapons production so that these facts may be taken into consideration in the debates on the Freeze and other nuclear arms control proposals. To present a thorough evaluation, CEP will look at both costs and benefits and at opportunity costs. Much of the information on the costs, employment impacts, and contracting networks for the new generation of nuclear weapons systems presented in this report is relevant to evaluating the potential economic effects of nuclear arms control proposals which are less inclusive than the nuclear Freeze.

Support for the Freeze

The Freeze is a serious public policy option with wide popular support. In state and local referenda, in public opinion polls, and in the US House of Representatives, the Freeze has been supported by a two to one margin over the past two years. [2] Its only major legislative setback was its rejection in the Senate by a 58 to 40 margin in November of 1983. Resolutions in support of the Freeze were passed at the Democratic Party mid-term issues convention and the recent biennial convention of the AFL-CIO. [3] Although opinion among experts from the defense, intelligence and foreign policy communities is divided on the issue, the Freeze is also gathering substantial support in these circles.

Logically, the political fate of the nuclear Freeze should rise or fall on its merits as a means of reducing the likelihood of a nuclear war. Unfortunately, political realities are not so pure. In its 1981 study, *The Iron Triangle,* CEP documents how weapons programs are often perpetuated for reasons having little to do with their strategic merits. [4] Rockwell International's ultimately successful campaign to revive the B-1 bomber is one of the clearest examples of the effectiveness of economic arguments in determining the fate of a weapons program. The company promoted the B-1 program by conducting an intensive grassroots lobbying campaign stressing the economic benefits of building the B-1 for each Congressional district and following through with regular campaign contributions for members of key Congressional committees and representatives of areas with Rockwell plants. In the 1981 vote restoring the program, 42 of 54 Rockwell supported members of the House of Representatives voted for the B-1. [5]

Rep. Joseph Addabbo, chairman of the House Appropriations Committee's subcommittee on the Department of Defense, described Rockwell's use of economic leverage in the following terms: "Rockwell is the best. I've had many members say: 'I have a plant with X number of jobs, and I just can't vote against that.' In effect, they've used Congressmen from those states as lobbyists." [6]

The economic effects of a Freeze, terminating not only the B-1, but MX and Trident missiles, Air-, Sea-, and Ground-Launched Cruise Missiles, the Pershing II missile, and production and testing of new nuclear warheads, will be wide ranging. This study will estimate these effects and seek to identify ways to minimize the economic disruption and maximize the economic benefits of a Freeze. Only when the economic ramifications of arms control proposals are considered from an informed perspective can the focus on their strategic merits be maintained.

In Chapter 1, CEP estimates how much of the projected expenditures for nuclear forces could be saved under a Freeze. It focuses both on year by year savings in warhead, missile, and bomber production over each of the next five years, and on potential budget savings through the end of this century. The potential benefits in budget savings must be weighed against the displacement of workers and loss of business in nuclear weapons systems production and testing.

Chapter 2 estimates the numbers and types of jobs that would be eliminated under a Freeze. It investigates the range of potential effects within the government-owned company-operated warhead development, production, and testing complex. The probable *net* effect of the Freeze on employment, since displacement in nuclear weapons production may be counterbalanced by other types of spending, is also discussed.

A more detailed picture of the opportunity costs of nuclear weapons system spending is presented in Chapter 3. How many jobs would alternative expenditures of these funds create? What types of programs and services could be supported for the cost of building the new generation of nuclear weapons? CEP focuses on three areas of national concern: 1) Restoration of key service programs in income maintenance, nutrition, education, and health and safety; 2) Public employment and public investment programs in housing, transportation and infrastructure development; and 3) Reduction of federal budget deficits. In addition to discussing alternative uses of *funds* currently devoted to nuclear weapons production, it discusses the implications of the *types* of resources engaged in these projects, particularly the disproportionate number of scientists and engineers involved. As we discuss briefly in Chapters II and III, Freeze savings may also be spent on additional conventional forces. Since there has been no clear consensus on which conventional forces (if any) should be increased under a bi-lateral nuclear weapons Freeze, CEP did not do a systematic assessment of the economic impacts of this option.

Chapter 4 documents the corporate role in nuclear weapons production by summarizing the most systematic information available on prime and subcontract awards for the production of each of the new nuclear armed missiles and the B-1 bomber program. The eight largest nuclear delivery vehicle contractors by volume of awards are discussed.

Even if the overall economic effects of a Freeze prove to be positive, particular workers and communities which depend on nuclear weapons system production will suffer a loss of jobs and income. Chapter 5 reviews national, state and local approaches to the problem of economic conversion, the transition from military to civilian production and employment. In each case the applicability of the approach to the economic adjustment problems raised by a Freeze is discussed.

Projections of the economic effect of proposed military programs (or their cancellation) are subject to a number of variables. Military plans change, affecting the numbers and types of particular weapons built. Cost and inflation projections change in the light of changes in weapons design and shifts in the overall economy. Working with the best available estimates for cost and employment impacts of the new generation of nuclear weapons systems, CEP is confident that our projections are as accurate as possible, given the current state of information. We have pointed to areas where further data is needed, and have been careful neither to overstate economic benefits nor underestimate economic problems posed by a nuclear Freeze. In doing so, we hope to stimulate a more informed debate on the economic implications of nuclear arms control.

Footnotes

1. The founding document and most explicit statement to date of the demands of the campaign for a bi-lateral US-USSR nuclear weapons Freeze is the "Call to Halt the Nuclear Arms Race", by Randall Forsberg of the Institute for Defense and Disarmament Studies in 1980. It opens as follows:

    "To improve national and international security, the United States and the Soviet Union should stop the nuclear arms race. Specifically, they should adopt a mutual Freeze on the testing, production, and deployment of nuclear weapons and of new missiles and bombers designed primarily to deliver nuclear weapons."

    The Reagan Administration's Strategic Arms Reduction Talks (START) position calls for reductions in the *numbers* of ballistic missile warheads deployed by the US and the Soviet Union, but it explicitly endorses "modernization" through building of new missiles such as the MX, Trident II, and Air-Launched Cruise Missiles. For a summary of the START position, see Casper W. Weinberger, Secretary of Defense, *Annual Report to Congress for FY 1984* (Washington: US GPO 1983), p. 57–58. Thus, a START *agreement* would have less impact on military industry than a Freeze agreement would.

2. In the CBS/New York Times polls of September 13, 1982 and June 20, 1983, 69% of the respondents expressed support for a mutual US-Soviet nuclear weapons Freeze. In referenda in 10 states and 38 cities and counties in the fall of 1982, over 60% of the 17 million who voted supported a bilateral Freeze (compilation by Nuclear Weapons Freeze Campaign National Clearinghouse, 4144 Lindell Blvd., St. Louis, MO 63108). On May 4, 1983, the House of Representatives passed a resolution for a bilateral Freeze by 278 to 149 (*New York Times*, May 5, 1983).

3. For the Democratic Party statement, see the final statement of the workshop on "Foreign Policy, Defense, and Arms Control" at the Democratic National Party Conference held in Philadelphia on June 26, 1982 (available from Democratic National Committee, Washington, DC). The decision to support the Freeze by the AFL-CIO biennial convention held in Hollywood, Florida in October of 1983 is reported in *California AFL-CIO News,* October 7, 1983, and the *AFL-CIO News,* October 15, 1983.

4. Gordon Adams, *The Iron Triangle: The Politics of Defense Contracting,* (New York: Council on Economic Priorities, 1981).

5. Gordon Adams, "The B-1: a Bomber for All Seasons?", (New York: Council on Economic Priorities 1982).

6. *US News and World Report,* July 11, 1983, "The B-1: When Pentagon, Politicians Joined Hands".

I

Budget Savings from a Nuclear Weapons Freeze

A Freeze on the production, testing, and deployment of new nuclear weapons systems would save *at least* $98 billion in scarce budgetary resources over the next five years, and over $380 billion by the year 2000. Cuts in spending on nuclear weapons, however, do not automatically lead to reduced military spending. Key Pentagon officials and even many Freeze supporters in Congress argue that a halt in nuclear weapons production would require further increases in spending on non-nuclear forces. (1) Other experts from the armed forces and Congress assert that existing US conventional forces are more than adequate for any reasonable strategy of defense. (2) In either case, a Freeze would precipitate a major shift in current plans for using government resources.

Estimates of the total costs of building, maintaining, and operating US nuclear forces over the next five years range from a low of $295 billion (according to Congressional Budget Office and Reagan Administration sources) to a high of more than $350 billion (according to independent estimates by the Washington based Center for Defense Information). (3) The differences in these estimates revolve primarily around two issues: 1) the costs of operations, maintenance, and support; 2) what percentage of Command, Control, Communications and Intelligence (C3I) spending is considered nuclear related. These differences are not crucial to ascertaining how much of the budget for nuclear forces, in the short term, would be saved under a nuclear Freeze. These short-term savings will come from foregoing procurement and testing funds for nuclear delivery vehicles (bombers and missiles) and nuclear warheads. Substantial savings in operating costs would only come if a Freeze led to substantial reductions in nuclear force levels.

Table I lists five year projections of budget outlay and budget authority savings realizable from the cancellation of the major nuclear weapons delivery vehicles: the B-1B bomber, the MX missile, the Air-, Sea- and Ground-Launched Cruise missiles, the Trident I and II missiles, and the Pershing II missile. The projected savings are conservative since they exclude classified programs (the Stealth bomber, the Advanced Cruise Missile, and the later years of the Pershing II program), programs still without year-by-year funding projections (the Midgetman missile program), and warhead production, which will be discussed separately.

Five year savings on the major delivery vehicles covered by a Freeze would be at least $75.9 billion in budget authority and $71.2 billion in budget outlays. Over 80 percent of the savings in both budget authority and outlays would come from a Freeze on the B-1 bomber, the MX missile, and the Trident II missile. The major savings in outlays would be realized in FY 1986 and after. The Stealth bomber, Advanced Cruise Missile program, and the newly proposed Midgetman missile would also be halted under a Freeze. If figures for outlays on these programs were available, estimates of savings in FY 1986 and beyond would be considerably higher.

A substantial source of potential budget savings from the Freeze not addressed in Table I is the cost of the Department of Energy's warhead production program. These savings will vary depending on how a Freeze is implemented at DoE facilities, and whether it includes a ban on the production of fissionable material for nuclear warheads as well as a ban on production of the actual bombs. Options range from halting the current expansion of plutonium production capacity and modernization of the warhead complex to shutting down many of the key facilities and leaving the remainder in a caretaker status. The most accurate means of estimating potential budget savings in the warhead complex is to examine the scope of the Department of Energy's "Atomic Energy Defense Activities", analyzing which of its functions are most likely to be terminated as part of a Freeze. Table II lists the latest Office of Management and Budget projections for "Atomic Energy Defense Activities" spending over the next five years.

Atomic Energy Defense activities will cost over $35 billion in both budget authority and outlays for the next five years, ranging from $6 to $8 billion in any given year. Not all activities would necessarily be stopped during a Freeze. In fact, only three of the ten major categories included under Atomic Energy Defense activities would be likely to yield major budget savings under a Freeze: Research, Development and Testing; Production and Surveillance; and Materials Production. These categories encompass the major tasks involved in the development, production, and testing of nuclear warheads. Table III lists the expenditures for major categories within the Atomic Energy Defense Activities budget for recent years. The three categories most likely to be affected by a Freeze have encompassed close to ¾ of all Atomic Energy Defense activities in recent years, and will likely maintain at least that proportion for the next five years. This indicates over $28 billion in savings for the next five years from a Freeze. Even allowing for continued maintenance of the existing nuclear stockpile, research on new weapons designs that stops short of actual development, and civilian related functions such as enrichment of uranium for nuclear power plants, potential savings from the warhead complex over the next five years could still approach $21 billion. This $21 billion added to the $75.9 billion savings on nuclear delivery vehicle production adds up to potential Freeze savings of $97.9 billion.

This savings represents roughly one-third of the costs of all nuclear weapons programs for the next five years and slightly more than 5 percent of total budget authority for "national defense" over the period, according to the latest Office of Management and Budget projections. (4)

There are other factors that could increase Freeze savings beyond this minimum figure. The first, and perhaps the most certain, is weapons system cost growth. Even with inflation factored into original estimates, the cost of 53 major weapon systems currently purchased by the US armed forces has nearly doubled since they originally entered development. The original projected cost of $339.8 billion to fully procure all 53 systems has jumped to $606.6 billion.(5) A leak from the Defense Resources Board, in early 1982, revealed that the full costs of buying all items included in the Reagan Administration's five year military program could exceed original estimtates by a full *$750 billion.*(6) Nuclear delivery vehicles, the most complex and costly systems, have conformed to or exceeded this general pattern of cost growth. The current $290 million unit cost of the B-1B bomber is nearly ten times the estimated cost of the first B-1 proposed in 1970.(7) The Ground-Launched Cruise Missile program has increased in projected costs by over 135 percent since 1977.(8) Although there are sharp disagreements over the principal sources of cost growth (increasing complexity, changes in design and capability, or plain and simple mismanagement), major weapons systems routinely cost two to three times their original estimates.

A second major contribution to Freeze savings could result from its potential effects on Congressional decisions on related weapons systems. With an effective Freeze in force, an array of related programs in strategic and civil defense, submarine construction, command, control and communications, satellite warfare, and ballistic missile defense R&D could be reconsidered and conceivably cancelled. Table IV summarizes the five year and long-term potential savings from systems strictly covered by a Freeze and related systems.

The $380 billion to $425 billion in funds that could be saved by halting production, testing, and deployment of nuclear systems over the next two decades represent significant resources for any nation, even one with the ample resources and diverse economic base of the United States. The economic effects of several possible alternative uses of these funds will be discussed in Chapter IV. But first we will analyze the potential effects of these cuts in nuclear weapon systems funding on employment.

Footnotes

1. The most comprehensive view put forward by the Democratic Party on the relationship of a Freeze to conventional arms spending came in the final statement of the workshop on "Foreign Policy, Defense, and Arms Control, 'American Security in the 1980's'", adopted as part of the 1982 Democratic National Party Conference held in Philadelphia on June 26, 1982. After endorsing the concept of a nuclear Freeze, representing a consensus of conservative, moderate, and liberal viewpoints within the party, the statement went on to endorse a conventional arms buildup:

    > *"The Democratic Party believes conventional military strength must be given priority national attention because these forces address the threats we are most likely to face, and effectively constituted, provide an alternative we must possess between defeat at one level of military power and escalation to another.*
    >
    > *The Democratic Party realizes that providing an effective conventional defense will make claims on our nation's resources. We believe that those who overlook the growth of Soviet military power and other military threats and who might imagine that freedom can be maintained without vigilance and sacrifice ignore our past and imperil our future."*

    Numerous Reagan Administration military officials have argued that a Freeze would require expanded conventional forces budgets. Perhaps the clearest expression of this point of view was presented by James P. Wade, Principal Deputy Undersecretary of Defense for Research and Engineering, before House Appropriations Committee hearings on the FY 1983 DoD budget:

    > *"We have heard comment about the so-called 'freeze proposal.' Everyone here appreciates the fact that if we ever made that mistake, accepted a Freeze, the cost in the sense of needed, additional conventional weapons would be very, very high indeed." (Department of Defense Appropriations for 1983, Hearings Before the Committee on Appropriations Subcommittee on the Department of Defense, US House of Representatives, Vol. 4, p. 549, US GPO 1982).*

2. Robert MacNamara, Secretary of Defense under President Johnson, and Cyrus Vance, Secretary of State under President Carter, submitted a plan for cutting $212 billion from the 1984 through 1988 Reagan military proposals to the House Appropriations Committee hearings on the FY 1984 budget which included substantial cuts in naval and land forces in addition to cuts in nuclear systems (DoD Appropriations for 1984, Hearings Before the Subcommittee on the Department of Defense, Committee on Appropriations, US House of Representatives, Part 9, p. 17, US GPO 1983). Independent analyses calling for a halt in the conventional forces buildup are contained in the Boston Study Group, *Winding Down: The Price of Defense* (W.H. Freeman, 1982), and the Center for Defense Information, "The Need for a Level Military Budget," *The Defense Monitor,* Volume XII, number 2 (Center for Defense Information, 1983).

3. Reagan Administration Principal Undersecretary of Defense for Research and Engineering James P. Wade asserted in hearings on the FY 1983 defense budget that strategic forces accounted for 15 percent of the DoD budget, "moving to 18 percent." (Department of Defense Appropriations for 1983, Hearings before the Subcommittee on the Department of Defense, U. S. House of Representatives, Washington, GPO, 1982, p. 549). Adding costs for Pershing and Cruise missiles in Europe and warhead production in the Department of Energy, this would imply a $300 billion commitment to nuclear forces over the next five years. This is compatible with the estimate of the Congressional Budget Office, *Modernizing US Strategic Offensive Forces: The Administration's Program and Alternatives* (Washington: GPO, 1983). Independent assessments by Randall Forsberg in *The Economic and Social Costs of the Nuclear Arms Race* (Brookline, MA: Institute for Defense and Disarmament Studies, 1981), former DoD budget analyst Earl Ravenal ("Anatomy of the Defense Budget," *Chicago Tribune,* May 10, 1982), and the Center for Defense Information ("More Bang, More Bucks: $450 Billion for Nuclear War," *The Defense Monitor,* Vol. XII, no. 7) have estimated that 20 to 22 percent of the defense budget goes toward nuclear forces, leading to estimates for the next five years of $320 to $350 billion.

4. US Office of Management and Budget, *Federal Government Finances,* February 1983. The 'national defense function', which includes the Department of Defense budget plus the Atomic Energy Defense Activities portion of the Department of Energy budget, is slated to consume $1.8 trillion in budget authority between 1984 and 1988.

5. Department of Defense, Office of the Assistant Secretary of Defense (Comptroller), "Selected Acquisition Reports Program Acquisition Summary as of June 30, 1983."

6. *Washington Post,* January 8, 1982.

7. Gordon Adams, "The B-1: A Bomber for All Seasons?," Council on Economic Priorities newsletter N82-2, February 1982; and DoD, June 1983 *Selected Acquisition Reports,* op. cit.

8. Department of Defense, SAR (see note 5).

Table I

Budget Savings as a Result of a Nuclear Freeze on Major Delivery Vehicles, FY 1984-1988
(Budget Authority and Outlays, $bn)

System	FY 1984	FY 1985	FY 1986	FY 1987	FY 1988	Five Year Total
B-1B Bomber						
Budget Authority	$6.9	$8.2	$6.0	$0.1	--	$21.2
Outlays	$3.7	$5.5	$6.7	$5.7	$4.5	$26.1
MX Missile						
Budget Authority	$6.6	$7.5	$6.6	$5.9	$3.4	$30.0
Outlays	$3.8	$5.4	$6.1	$5.7	$5.0	$26.0
Trident II Missile						
Budget Authority	$1.5	$2.3	$3.1	$3.7	$4.3	$14.9
Outlays	$0.9	$1.7	$2.3	$2.6	$3.0	$10.5
Trident I Missile						
Budget Authority	$0.6	$0.2	$0.1	$0.1	$0.1	$1.1
Outlays	$0.7	$0.6	$0.4	$0.2	$0.2	$2.1
Pershing II Missile						
Budget Authority	$0.5	$0.4	(86-88 Pershing II BA Classified)			$0.9
Outlays	$0.2	$0.3	$0.3	$0.2	--	$1.0
Air-Launched Cruise Missile						
Budget Authority	$0.2	$0.2	$0.2	$0.2	$0.1	$0.9
Outlays	less than $0.1	$0.3	$0.2	$0.2	$0.2	$0.9

Source: Congressional Budget Office, unpublished estimates based on the DoD Five Year Defense Program, June 1983.

Continued

System	FY 1984	FY 1985	FY 1986	FY 1987	FY 1988	Five Year Total
Sea-Launched Cruise Missile (Tomahawk)						
Budget Authority	$0.6	$0.9	$1.0	$1.1	$1.2	$4.8
Outlays	$0.4	$0.6	$0.6	$0.5	$0.2	$2.3
Ground-Launched Cruise Missile						
Budget Authority	$0.8	$0.6	$0.6	$0.1	--	$2.1
Outlays	$0.4	$0.6	$0.6	$0.5	$0.2	$2.3
Year by Year Savings, All Systems						
Budget Authority	$17.7	$20.3	$17.9	$11.2	$9.1	$75.9
Outlays	$10.1	$15.0	$17.2	$15.6	$13.3	$71.2

Note on terms and methodology: Budget authority is "authority provided by law to enter into obligations that will result in immediate or future outlays involving Federal Government funds." Outlays represent spending in a given fiscal year, and may be the result of current or prior year decisions: "Outlays...flow in part from unexpended balances of prior-year budget authority and in part from budget authority provided for in the year in which the money is spent." (Definitions are from US General Accounting Office, *A Glossary of Terms Used in the Federal Budget Process*, Washington, US GPO, 1981.) The original estimates provided by the Congressional Budget Office tracked only proposed budget authority for FY 1984–88 and how that authority would be spent. CEP added estimates for additional budget outlays in 1984-87 flowing from authorizations in the FY 1980 through FY 1983 period, using figures from the Department of Defense, *Program Acquisition Costs by Weapon System*, and Congressional Budget Office estimates of how defense procurement and research and development budget authority translate into outlays.

Table II

Savings from a Freeze, Atomic Energy Defense
Activities, FY 1984 Through FY 1988
(Billions of Current Year Dollars)

	FY 1984	FY 1985	FY 1986	FY 1987	FY 1988	Five Year Total
Budget Authority	$6.8	$8.0	$8.0	$8.1	$7.8	$38.7
Budget Authority Savings from a Freeze[a]	$3.8	$4.5	$4.5	$4.6	$4.4	$21.8
Outlays	$6.4	$7.4	$7.7	$8.2	$8.0	$37.7
Outlay Savings from a Freeze[a]	$3.6	$4.2	$4.3	$4.6	$4.5	$21.2

a   Authority and outlay savings were calculated by taking 75% of the portion of Atomic Energy Defense Activities which goes directly for R&D, testing, and production of warheads (see table III of this chapter for further details).

Source: Office of Management and Budget, *Federal Government Finances*, February 1983.

Table III

Funding of Department of Energy Defense Activities by Function, with Freeze-Related Proportion of FY 1984 Request
(Thousands of Dollars)

	FY 1982 Actual	FY 1983 Estimate	FY 1984 Request	% of 1984 Request
Inertial Confinement Fusion	$ 209,062	$ 189,750	$ 151,800	--
Research and Development and Testing[a]	1,103,280	1,184,800	1,380,080	20.4
Production and Surveillance[a]	1,596,733	1,900,900	2,337,315	34.4
Program Direction -- Weapons	47,258	50,091	55,930	--
Verification and Control Technology	52,000	53,900	61,650	--
Materials Production[a]	955,612	1,202,760	1,485,300	21.9
Defense Waste and By-Products Management	377,893	518,729	611,500	--
Nuclear Materials Safe-guards and Security	47,219	47,360	52,000	--
Naval Reactors Development	495,920	526,910	613,000	--
Security Investigations	23,600	28,500	29,500	--
Total, Atomic Energy Defense Activities	$4,904,577	$5,703,700	$6,778,075	76.7[b]

a   These are the main categories of Atomic Energy Defense Activities which would yield budget savings under a nuclear Freeze.

b   Freeze-related percentage of 1984 total.

Source: Department of Energy *Congressional Budget Request FY 1984: Volume 1, Atomic Energy Defense Activities.*

Table IV

Potential Budget Savings from a Nuclear Freeze, FY 1984–88 and Beyond

	FY 1984-88 Savings ($ billion)	And Beyond . . . ($ billion)
SYSTEMS DEFINITELY INCLUDED IN A FREEZE		
MX Missile[a]	$30.0	$70 billion through year 2000
B-1B Bomber	21.2	Depends on whether additional B-1s beyond first 100 are bought (see Stealth bomber)
Trident I Missile	1.1	Program phasing out in favor of Trident II
Trident II Missile	14.9	$35.4 billion
Air-Launched Cruise Missile	0.9	Minimum total of $5.3 including later buy of the Advanced Cruise Missile
Sea-Launched Cruise Missile	4.8	$8.5 billion
Ground-Launched Cruise Missile	2.1	$2.2 billion
Pershing II Missile[b]	0.9	$1.4 billion
Nuclear Warhead Production, Development and Testing, Including Production of Fissionable Materials	21.8	No estimates available beyond 1988, but at current rates of $6 to 8 billion/yr, savings could run over $100 billion by year 2000
TOTAL	$97.7	245 billion[c]
SYSTEMS NOW IN R & D WHOSE DEVELOPMENT AND PRODUCTION WOULD BE STOPPED IN THE NEXT FIVE YEARS		
Midgetman Small ICBM		$107 billion for procurement and 20 year life-cycle
Stealth Bomber		$30 billion through 1991
TOTAL		$137 billion

Continued

ADDITIONAL SAVINGS ON RELATED
SYSTEMS WHICH COULD BE REALIZED
ONCE A FREEZE TAKES EFFECT

Ballistic Missile Defense	$10 to 25 billion
Strategic Air Defense	$2.5 billion through 1987
Command, Control and Communications for a Prolonged Nuclear Conflict	$7 billion through 1987
Trident Submarine	$11 billion for remaining 8 submarines in 20 sub program[d]
TOTAL ADDITIONAL SAVINGS	$30 to 45 billion

The format and original set of data for this table were developed by Steve Daggett of the Coalition for a New Foreign and Military Policy and Ed Glennon of SANE for the flyer "Economic Benefits of a Freeze."

a   MX costs reflect cost of Dense Pack basing mode which has since been rejected in favor of placing 100 MX missiles in existing silos. Cost differences for the two basing modes of several billion dollars are expected, but the basic costs for production of missiles would be the same under either plan.

b   Pershing II missile expenditures for 1986 and beyond are classified. This is a minimum estimate.

b   The total for beyond 1988 *includes* the $97.7 billion that could potentially be saved in the 1984–1988 period.

c   The most recent *Selected Acquisition Reports* documents from the Pentagon (as of December 31, 1982) have excluded the costs of the final eight Trident submarines. However, since no change in strategic policy has been announced to coincide with this change in accounting, this savings table assumes a twenty submarine program. Further savings could potentially accrue if some of the submarines already authorized but yet to go into production were de-funded.

Sources: Congressional Budget Office, unpublished estimates on five year weapons costs, and a May 1983 study, *Modernizing US Strategic Offensive Forces: The Administration's Program and Alternatives;* Office of the Assistant Secretary of Defense, Comptroller, *Selected Acquisition Reports* as of March 31, 1983; and US Office of Management and Budget, *Federal Government Finances,* February 1983 and *Aviation Week and Space Technology,* October 12, 1981.

11

II

Effects of a Nuclear Freeze on Employment

Just as potential budget savings are its most visible economic benefit, the displacement of workers currently engaged in nuclear weapons production is the most important economic problem posed by a nuclear Freeze. Some 600,000 workers are involved in the production of nuclear warheads, nuclear delivery vehicles, and related support equipment.[1] These numbers will grow in step with the increased investment in nuclear forces planned for the next five years.[2]

Actual employment effects of a nuclear Freeze will not be as widespread or as negative as many assume:

- A net increase of 50,000 to 150,000 jobs nationwide would result if budget savings from a Freeze are spent on civilian government purchases or returned to the taxpayers.[3]

- Job displacement will be highly concentrated geographically, since ten states receive over 94 percent of the prime contracts for missiles and bombers covered by a Freeze. Thirty-eight states would incur little or no economic displacement.[4]

- Displaced jobs will fall disproportionately into professional and technical job categories with relatively low unemployment rates. Guided missile production, which will account for most of the Freeze cutbacks, employs *six times* as many professional and technical workers as the average manufacturing industry, and only *one-third* as many production workers.[5]

Although these findings indicate that employment under a Freeze could actually rise, the problem of finding new employment for tens of thousands of displaced workers and new economic activities for dependent communities remains.

How many workers would actually be displaced by a nuclear Freeze? Table I provides estimates of total jobs displaced by a Freeze implemented in any of the next five years. There are a number of limitations to this data. A Freeze initially only affects the production, testing, and deployment of a specified set of new warhead, missile, and bomber programs. Only a portion of the workforce in the nuclear weapons industry, therefore, would be displaced by its implementation. The extent of displacement depends upon the timing of a Freeze and whether research funds are cut, remain at current projections, or increase. The Department of Energy's contractor-operated warhead production and testing complex is another area of uncertainty. Definitive estimates are difficult to make because of the overlapping of military and energy research functions with testing and production of warheads at the major facilities of the complex.

At the height of the nuclear weapons production cycle, with the most severe cutbacks possible as a result of a Freeze, 350,000 workers would be displaced, less than 0.4 percent of the total US workforce. This includes direct *and* indirect employment in missile and bomber production, and direct employment in warhead production and testing.`

Nuclear Weapons Systems Spending: Fewer Jobs

The Bureau of Labor Statistics (BLS) input-output model of the US economy offers one of the most precise methods available for measuring the relative employment impact of various types of spending. The model captures both direct employment in any given industry and the *indirect* employment which spending in that industry stimulates in all other industries supplying components and materials to it.(6) Later in this chapter, the issue of additional employment induced by spending of employee wages in the direct and indirect supplier industries will also be addressed. Table II presents the most recent BLS estimates of employment requirements per $1 billion spent on guided missiles, aircraft, radio and communications equipment, and other important manufacturing and service activities.

The table demonstrates that major nuclear weapons related industries create: 1) from two-thirds to one-half as many jobs per billion dollars spent as apparel manufacture, steel production, or motor vehicle manufacturing; and 2) one-half to one-third as many jobs as equivalent spending for hospital or educational services. In fact, expenditures for sophisticated guided missile systems such as the MX and Trident create fewer jobs than most forms of civilian spending. The two most recent studies of the impact of military procurement on employment were conducted by Employment Research Associates and the Congressional Budget Office. They found that general government spending on weapons creates between 25,000 and 28,000 jobs per billion dollars spent. This compares favorably with the 21,000 jobs per billion dollars created by guided missile spending. If savings from a Freeze were spent on either civilian government programs or procurement of non-nuclear weapons, there would probably be a net increase in overall employment.(7) To fully assess the employment impacts of a Freeze it is necessary to determine which other industries beyond guided missile and aircraft production would be affected.

Industrial Sectors
Affected by a Freeze

Direct employment in the production of missiles and bombers is only part of the story, since more than half of the total jobs created are in the indirect supplier industries. The same BLS employment requirements tables, presenting relative effects on total employment of different forms of spending, can be used to specify industries receiving the largest amount of indirect employment. This is essential for assessing the full industrial impact of a Freeze. In the absence of systematic government or industry reporting on subcontracting networks for systems such as the MX and B-1, it offers a method for estimating nuclear weapons system spending beyond the level of prime contractors.(8)

Table III shows the indirect employment in the top industries supplying goods and services for guided missiles and aircraft production, and the percentage of indirect employment accounted for by each industry. Of the 156 supplier industries tracked in the input-output tables, six suppliers account for more than half of the indirect employment generated by spending on guided missiles. Eight industries account for nearly half of the indirect employment generated by aircraft production. Aircraft is the largest indirect supplier industry in the production of complete guided missiles, and electronic components and radio and communications equipment are among the top supplying industries of both aircraft and guided missiles.

Beyond these industrial categories, major supplier industries are "eating and drinking places," "business services," "hotels and lodging places," and "retail trade." This reflects the tremendous amount of effort exerted by military contractors on lobbying, bids and proposals, and public relations efforts to maintain a foothold in the government subsidized market for military goods and services.(9) In fact, an analysis of aircraft and missile production indicates that cuts in these programs are likely to result in more layoffs of waiters, accountants and sales clerks than production workers. While layoffs in these areas are equally serious, these job categories are more widely dispersed throughout the national economy, and offer a better chance of re-employment as the economy improves.

These findings are consistent with a more detailed analysis by Gail Shields in CEP's *Misguided Expenditure: An Analysis of the MX Missile System.*(10) To test the assertion that spending on guided missiles such as the MX stimulates "high technology" manufacturing sectors, CEP compared the impact on capital goods and other manufacturing industries of spending on guided missile production versus five alternatives: mass transit, solar energy, railroads, public utilities, and housing. Table IV summarizes the findings. It shows that guided missile production had a smaller secondary impact on manufacturing industries than any of the alternatives and a much smaller impact on capital goods industries.

Even within direct employment in the guided missile and aircraft industries, there are relatively few production jobs. The distribution by type of jobs for missile and bomber production is weighted heavily toward technical and scientific personnel.

Technical Skills and Nuclear Weapons Production

The relatively low job creation capacity of nuclear weapons system spending is directly related to the disproportionate share of scientists, engineers, professional, and technical workers employed in this area. Table V demonstrates that the three sectors most closely tied to nuclear weapons production—guided missiles, aircraft, and communication equipment—employ three to six times as many professional and technical workers and four to ten times as many engineers as the average manufacturing industry. These nuclear-related categories also employ substantially more professional and technical personnel than other major procurement categories such as ordnance and shipbuilding.

The high proportion of technical personnel in nuclear weapons related industries is matched by the low proportion of production workers: operatives and laborers make up only 29·percent of the aircraft manufacturing work force and less than *12 percent* in the guided missile industry. Operatives and laborers comprise over 51 percent of the work force in the average manufacturing industry.

The mix of job categories involved in the production of nuclear weapons systems has signficant implications. In December 1982, when the national unemployment rate had reached its post World War II peak of 10.8 percent, unemployment for professional and technical workers was only 3.7 percent, while operatives and laborers had an average unemployment rate of 20.4 percent.(11) Because nuclear systems production provides relatively fewer jobs for those most in need of employment, a Freeze would have a much less severe displacement effect than cutbacks in the average industry. However, there would still be unique problems of retraining and re-adjustment of scientists and engineers used to working in the performance conscious, high cost realm of military production. This transition would probably be eased by the generally high demand for scientific and engineering talent.

The Impact of a Freeze on the Warhead Production Complex

The specialized nature of nuclear warhead production requires it to be analyzed separately. A detailed review of the Department of Energy's government-owned, company-operated research, development, testing and production complex for nuclear weapons is necessary. Since there is little data available on the indirect industrial impacts of warhead production, this analysis covers only direct production at DOE facilities and some offsite employment under contract.

From research through production, all stages of nuclear warhead work are conducted within a nationwide complex of over 50 Department of Energy research and development field facilities employing more than 108,000 people as of 1981.(12) Over 40 percent of this employment is centered in multi-program laboratories that perform both energy and nuclear weapons research, development, and testing. Another 40 percent is devoted to production of special nuclear materials (for use in warhead production and fueling nuclear reactors) or in the fabrication and assembly of nuclear weapons. The remaining 20 percent are devoted to single purpose, program dedicated laboratories working on everything from research on reactors for submarines to solar energy. These program dedicated facilities are the least likely to suffer cutbacks as a result of a Freeze.

Table VI demonstrates that roughly 60 percent or 65,000 of the employees in the DoE's R & D field facilities are either scientists and engineers or professional and technical workers. However, as the breakdown by type of facility indicates, this figure is an average. It includes a ratio of 70 percent technical workers at the multi-program and program-dedicated laboratories and 40 percent at the nuclear materials production and nuclear weapons component fabrication facilities. Bear-

16

ing this in mind, the direct employment in the nuclear warhead complex uses nearly as high a proportion of technical employees as guided missile production (over 55 percent professional and technical).* To estimate which of the employees in this entire complex are most likely to be affected by a Freeze, it is necessary to determine more precisely how the facilities primarily responsible for warhead research, testing and production would be treated.

Even under a full Freeze on fissionable materials production for weapons and construction of new warheads, the potential job impacts at DoE facilities could vary widely. The history and original rationale of much of the current defense *and* energy workloads at the DoE facilities is tied directly to the function of the complex as the center of nuclear weapons and naval nuclear propulsion work in the United States. If the Freeze halts the building and designing of new nuclear warheads for years to come, it could undermine the rationale for the heavy bias of DoE R&D work towards nuclear energy. The result could be either a move into more work on other energy sources or a drastic reduction in Federal energy R&D programs.

There are, however, several more immediate issues that could affect the size of the DoE work force under a Freeze. The distinction between research or development and testing personnel at the facilities will affect the number of layoffs, since research is not strictly banned by a Freeze. Also, how officials in the Department of Defense and Energy and heads of the facilities treat the Freeze—a pause in the arms race or a step towards further bilateral weapons reductions—may affect how hard they will lobby for large staffing levels. CEP's estimate of between 45,000 and 53,000 displaced workers in the entire complex is based on the following assumptions: 1) no facilities will be completely shut down; 2) research funding will not change dramatically to compensate for cuts in production and testing; and 3) all positions directly tied to weapons production, development, or testing will be terminated, but all nuclear energy research will be preserved at current levels.

To show the worst possible displacement effects of a Freeze, job loss figures cited at the beginning of this chapter were at the high end of the range for the warhead complex. Table VII presents estimates, by facility, for employment impacts at each of the major nuclear materials production facilities, warhead fabrication and assembly sites, and testing sites. Effects on weapons research laboratories are treated separately in Table VIII.

Estimated displacement of workers at the materials production, com-

*The category "professional and technical" in Table V *includes* scientists and engineers, whereas the DoE statistics in table six list 'scientists and engineers' and 'other professional and technical' as separate categories. The two table VI categories *combined* are comparable to the 'professional and technical category in Table V.

ponent fabrication, final assembly, and testing sites listed in Table VII accounts for 48,000 positions. This is well under one-half of the total employment at the DoE's research and development field facilities. The percentage of the work force affected at each site ranges from 12 percent at Idaho National Engineering Laboratories (primarily naval nuclear propulsion programs), to 50 percent at Hanford Nuclear Reservation (actively involved in nuclear energy programs), to 90 percent at the major component and assembly plants. These plants will require some maintenance or caretaker presence. The 90 percent layoff assumption is in keeping with CEP's attempt to gauge the maximum displacement affect of a Freeze short of total shutdown of any facilities. The DoE's three uranium enrichment facilities at Piketon, Ohio, Paducah, Kentucky, and Oak Ridge, Tennessee are missing from the list since their primary current role is the enrichment of fuel for nuclear utilities. Although the enrichment plants were originally constructed to produce highly enriched uranium for the atomic and hydrogen bomb programs, according to the DoE's Office of Nuclear Materials Production, "The gaseous diffusion plants have not enriched uranium for the operation of the [plutonium] production reactors or fabrication of weapons components since the early 1960s."(13) CEP treated these plants as relatively invulnerable to adverse short-term impacts from a Freeze even though they could be used in the future for production of highly enriched uranium for weapons.

Effects on Warhead Design Laboratories

The major laboratories engaged in nuclear weapons research and design—Sandia Laboratories and Los Alamos Scientific Laboratories in New Mexico, and Lawrence Livermore Laboratories in Livermore, California—are technically designated as "multi-program laboratories." These labs are also involved with numerous other military and energy projects. Two other "multi-program" laboratories—the Savannah River Laboratory and Oak Ridge National Laboratories—are located on the same sites as major nuclear materials and nuclear weapons component production facilities and would be affected by a Freeze. The bulk of their work flows from the needs of nuclear weapons programs. However, even these more narrowly focused laboratories have programs in nuclear energy, environmental assessment, radioactive waste management, and fossil and alternative energy research. These programs could logically continue even during a nuclear Freeze.

The fate of employees and programs at the nuclear weapons laboratories, more than in any other area we have analyzed, is an open question. The "Call to Halt the Nuclear Arms Race," the most detailed definition of the nuclear Freeze campaign, speaks of a "total Freeze on

18

nuclear weapons testing, production and deployment (and by implication, development)."(14) At a public hearing held in September of 1982 by the Federation of American Scientists, Randall Forsberg, the author of the "Call to Halt the Nuclear Arms Race," gave her perspective on the handling of warhead research under a Freeze:

> Dr. von Hippel: . . . I think one can conceive of mothballing a production facility and restarting it within a reasonable length of time.
> I think it would be much more difficult to mothball R&D facilities, such as national weapons labs . . . and, if a Freeze should fall apart, be able to put it together again quickly.

> Ms. Forsberg: . . . I do think that it would be important under a Freeze regime to maintain expertise on how nuclear weapons work. I don't think there is any security need of the United States or the West which requires, at this point, after thirty years of making nuclear warheads, that we be able to design new types of nuclear warheads with enhanced radiation, a different physical configuration, a different amount of blast, or a different proportion of heat.
> There are a great variety of designs—at least 80 different types of warheads have gotten as far as prototype.
> These many designs of different sizes and effects of nuclear weapons are more than adequate for the future of U.S. security, regardless of anything the Soviet Union might do.
> . . . A staff of people who understand how nuclear warheads work can be maintained without a large research and development operation, through giving them high salaries and related technical activities in the nuclear area.(15)

Richard Garwin, a nuclear physicist involved in nuclear weapons research and a fellow at IBM's Watson Research Center, also implied the possibility of significantly reducing the nuclear weapons research work force under a Freeze at the same hearings:

> Ambassador Fisher: . . . With respect to a comprehensive test ban, one of the great concerns expressed is that all of our scientists will get bored and will go out and help make better television sets, while the Soviets will be sitting around in a sort of hot lab someplace in Smolensk ready to resume at the drop of a hat. . . . In your experience with Soviet scientists, do you think they can maintain a stable of nonproductive scientists sitting around waiting to do something they cannot do?

> Dr. Garwin: I have worked for many years part-time at one of the nuclear weapons labs here, and I think we could do just as well as they could. There are all kinds of interesting problems in nuclear weapons. And one can do astrophysics, one can do inertially confined fusion, which has much in common with nuclear weapons. . . . It is not true, in my opinion, that the Soviet Union would have an advantage in this way. But we would have to pay attention to keeping laboratories (one laboratory: it is not at all clear that we need two laboratories in the nuclear design business) staffed with good people . . . (16)

Table VIII presents a range of estimates for employment losses at nuclear weapons laboratories.

Undoubtedly there will be pressures from within the laboratories, the Department of Energy, and the Department of Defense to maintain funding and staffing at the weapons laboratories at the highest levels possible.

A 1980 joint Department of Defense/Department of Energy study of weapons stockpile requirements over the next twenty years focused on the need to maintain a 'warm production base' for nuclear weapons and stressed the importance of trained personnel. The study points out that, "While discussions of production capability often emphasize facilities and equipment, they should not overlook trained and experienced personnel. Personnel considerations are particularly important and are often the limiting factor during periods of rapidly changing workloads."(17) Recent congressional testimony by General William Hoover, head of the DoE's Office of Military Applications, stresses that the decline in weapons research, development and testing personnel since the early 1970s is a problem that must be overcome. Table IX details General Hoover's presentation of the trend in nuclear weapons R&D employment.

The Lawrence Livermore Laboratory made this same argument most forcefully in its most recent *Institutional Plan*. It asserts that, "This modest [FY 1981 and 1982] increase in funding has fostered significant improvements; personnel morale and determination have been revitalized, and this has directly resulted in some exciting developments in nuclear weapons. Unfortunately current funding levels will not permit appropriate exploitation of these developments. To continue our support of the current stockpile and to vigorously pursue new designs the RD &T operating budget must be increased by 40 percent by FY 1985; and the existing equipment and facility deficiencies must be corrected."(18)

Weapons program officials now argue that funding and personnel are substantially below the necessary level to pursue the current stockpile buildup. It is quite likely that they will fight to maintain at least the existing levels of personnel and technology to allow for a resumption of weapons testing and development if a Freeze breaks down.

In fact, when ratification of a Comprehensive Test Ban appeared possible during the Carter Administration, Lawrence Livermore's *Institutional Plan* for 1978-1984 stressed the *additional funds* that would be required if there was an end to nuclear warhead testing:

> There are a number of steps and actions, allowed within a CTB, which should accompany any test ban treaty to minimize and delay undesirable technological consequences of the treaty. These safeguards include the maintenance of two strong design laboratories, enough funding to provide the increased calculational ability required, programs to retain and exercise

the essential cadre of weapons designers and supporting technologies. In view of our need to maintain a reliable stockpile, to design warheads for new military systems, and to carry on an aggressive advanced development program, we are dismayed to see an actual decline in the Laboratory's weapons budget dollars from FY 1978 to FY 1979 with a decrease of 7–8% in purchasing power.(19)

Regional Concentration of Nuclear Systems Employment

Nuclear weapons production affected by a Freeze is heavily concentrated geographically. This is most obvious in the case of guided missile production. Seven states accounted for between 77 and 89 percent of total guided missile industry employment in 1981, with California accounting for nearly two-thirds of the industry's work force. Table X documents the extreme concentration of employment as of 1981.

The employment figures in Table X cover work on everything from small tactical missiles to the MX ICBM. However, in terms of funding from the Pentagon, roughly half of the money authorized in recent years has been for missiles that will serve as nuclear weapons delivery vehicles.(20) There are, at this time, no employment figures available for each type of guided missile. Statistics on contracts to different states by type of missile give some sense of which states would most likely be seriously affected under a Freeze. Table XI lists the states with the highest levels of prime contract awards for missiles that would be taken out of production under a Freeze. Funding for guided missiles affected by a Freeze is highly concentrated in one area for every system. The top six states account for over two-thirds of total prime contracts awarded for these systems in FY 1982, and the top ten states account for over 79 percent. When B-1 bomber contracts are factored in, concentration of all nuclear delivery vehicle contracts is even greater: the top five states received over 76 percent of prime contracts, and the top ten states received 94 percent of all awards.

Potential problems posed by Freeze related cutbacks in military contracting vary considerably, depending upon the relative size of the defense industry and the manufacturing base in each affected state. For example, the $2 billion in awards for nuclear missiles to California in 1982 represents less than 10 percent of the $22.7 billion in total Department of Defense prime contract awards to that state for the year.(21) By comparison, Utah's $180 million in MX prime contracts represents just over half of total DoD awards to that state, and Colorado's $452 million in MX contracts accounts for 42 percent of total Pentagon awards to the state in 1982. California's civilian labor force of over 12 million people is nearly eight times as large as Colorado's (1.6 million) and over 17 times as large as Utah's (668,000).(22) With their diversified manufacturing and high technology industries, the possibilities for absorbing laid off engineering and manufacturing personnel in the Los Angeles or Denver areas is greater than in the case of cutbacks in MX work at the Hercules and Thiokol plants in Utah. However, even in California's industrial economy, special problems of readjustment will occur.

Projected Regional Employment Breakdown of B-1B Production

There is no systematic data currently available to permit a thorough analysis of the regional concentration of bomber and warhead production affected by a Freeze.

The B-1B bomber is a relatively small part of overall aircraft production. The only available data on regional employment patterns for this program comes from the lead associate prime contractor, Rockwell International. The firm estimates that 60,000 jobs will be created. This includes Rockwell's facilities in El Segundo and Palmdale, California and Columbus, Ohio; General Electric's engine facility outside of Cincinnati, Ohio; Boeing's Seattle, Washington, and Wichita, Kansas locations for offensive avionics work; and Eaton's AIL Division, Deer Park, Long Island site for defensive avionics. The 60,000 figure represents the peak of B-1B production in FY 1986 for each of the associate prime contractors. It does not include the full direct and indirect employment systematically as in an input-output analysis.(23) Although the bulk of B-1 jobs will be in the Los Angeles, Seattle, Cincinnati, and Long Island area locations of the four associate prime contractors, thousands of other jobs will be distributed across the country as part of the 5,200 company supplier network for the system. Reports by Rockwell International on the original B-1 program released in 1976 indicate that 15 separate states would obtain 1,000 jobs or more per year as a result of B-1 prime and subcontracts. This report also indicated that over 60 percent of the jobs would be in the four states where the major associate prime contractors are located.(24)

Many members of Congress assert that Rockwell has consciously spread its supplier network as widely as possible to insure political support in a majority of Congressional districts. House Armed Services Committee member Patricia Schroeder (D-CO), a B-1 opponent, stated: "The B-1 is a classic. From the standpoint of efficiency, to try to make a nuclear weapon in as many districts as possible is nuts, but from a lobbying standpoint, it's incredibly sophisticated."(25)

Will a Nuclear Freeze
Increase Unemployment?

This chapter has focused on the numbers and types of jobs that would be eliminated as a result of a nuclear Freeze. This approach was taken in order to give an honest appraisal of the potential economic costs of a Freeze, *and* to provide some of the information necessary for planning the implementation of a Freeze with a minimum of economic disruption. However, it is important to point out that even if close to 350,000 workers are *displaced* as a result of a halt in nuclear weapons systems production, there could be a *net increase* in total employment nationwide. If the cut in nuclear weapons spending is compensated by civilian government spending, spending on conventional weapons, or by a tax cut allowing consumers more spendable income, there would be a net increase in total nationwide employment. A study of the B-1 bomber program by Chase Econometrics, commissioned by principal prime contractor Rockwell International, confirms this point. Table XII presents Chase's findings on the net job increases offered by each of the alternatives for the key years of the program. Although this analysis was applied to the original B-1 bomber program of the late 1970s, it remains the most detailed analysis of its relative employment impact. Combining a sophisticated multi-equation model to trace overall effects on supply and demand of different expenditure patterns and an input-output model to measure employment impacts by industry, Chase found that either a tax cut, a housing program, or a welfare/public works program of equivalent size would create more total employment than building the B-1 bomber. The Chase methodology captures not only direct and indirect employment, but the overall net effects, including induced employment supported by employees in military industry spending their wages.

Chase's findings are supported by a recent study by the Employment Research Associates (ERA), *Destructive Investment: Nuclear Weapons and Economic Decline*. ERA compares the jobs created in 1981 as a result of $20 billion in spending on nuclear weapons and primary delivery and support systems with the number of jobs this $20 billion might have created had it been returned to consumers through a tax cut. Jobs foregone in consumer oriented industries such as residential construction, motor vehicles, and textiles and apparel far outnumbered the jobs produced by nuclear weapons spending. The net increase from a tax cut in 1981 would have been 270,000 jobs according to ERA. CEP has applied the ERA findings to the case of a Freeze in 1984, and estimated that turning the $13.7 billion in outlay savings back to the taxpayers could increase overall employment by as much as 150,000 jobs.(26)

The most recent Congressional Budget Office (CBO) report on *Defense Spending and the Economy* offers further confirmation that a shift from weapons *procurement* to civilian government purchases would result in a net increase in employment. Since a Freeze primarily affects the weapons procurement portion of the DoD and DoE budgets, this is a most relevant comparison for determining overall employment effects. The CBO found that while an additional $10 billion in civilian government purchases would create 250,000 jobs, an equal increase in defense purchases from industry would create only 210,000 jobs.(27) Using CBO's calculations, a shift of budget savings from a Freeze to civilian programs in 1984 could result in a net increase of 50,000 jobs this year and larger increases in years to come. Like the Chase study of the B-1, the CBO's study used a complex econometric model which accounts for induced employment as well as direct and indirect employment caused by a given expenditure.

Footnotes

1. No direct survey of the number of workers involved in nuclear warhead and delivery vehicle production has ever been done. Randall Forsberg did an estimate based on the percentage of weapons procurement and R&D spending going to nuclear weapons systems in *The Economic and Social Costs of the Nuclear Arms Race* (full citation in Chapter 2, note 3) of 550,000 workers as of 1981. David McFadden prepared a similar estimate from Pentagon contract listings of 600,000 as of 1983, in *The Freeze Economy* (Mountain View, CA: Mid-Peninsula Conversion Project, 1983). The Pentagon's estimate of total employment in defense industry positions as of 1983 was 2.7 million (Office of the Assistant Secretary of Defense, Comptroller, *National Defense Budget Estimates for FY 1984).*

2. Sources and discussions of these estimates of spending on nuclear forces are described in Chapter 1, footnote 3.

3. These estimates are from the Congressional Budget Office, *Defense Spending and the Economy,* February 1983, and Marion Anderson, Jeb Brugmann, and George Erikcek, *Destructive Investment: Nuclear Weapons and Economic Decline* (Lansing: Employment Research Associates, 1983). The last section of this chapter explains how these estimates were derived.

4. See Table XI of this chapter for documentation of this point.

5. According to the US Department of Labor, Bureau of Labor Statistics, *Supplement to Employment and Earnings, Revised Establishment Data,* June 1982, production workers accounted for 28% of employment in the guided missile industry compared with the 71% share of production workers in employment in the average manufacturing industry.

6. For detailed descriptions of input-output methodology, see Gail Shields,"Input-Output Analysis of Guided Missile Production," in David Gold, et. al., *Misguided Expenditure: An Analysis of the Proposed MX Missile System* (New York: Council on Economic Priorities, 1981) and Gail Shields, "The Economic Impact of the MX Missile," Science for the People, September/October 1982.

7. Marion Anderson, Jeb Brugmann, and George Erikcek, *The Price of the Pentagon: The Industrial and Commercial Impact of the 1981 Military Budget* (Lansing: Employment Research Associates, 1982) and Congressional Budget Office, *op. cit.*

8. The most detailed public accounting of subcontract awards is US Department of Defense, Washington Headquarters Services, "Geographic Distribution of Subcontract Awards, FY 1979." By its own admission, this survey covered data on only 38% of the dollar value of DoD subcontracts during that year.

9. For background on defense contractor lobbying and entertainment practices, see Gordon Adams, *The Iron Triangle: The Politics of Defense Contracting* (New York: Council on Economic Priorities, 1981).

10. David Gold, et. al., *op. cit.* See note 6.

11. US Department of Labor, Bureau of Labor Statistics, *The Employment Situation: December 1982,* January 7, 1983, Tables A-1, A-2, and A-5. Originally cited in Robert W. DeGrasse, Jr. *Military Expansion, Economic Decline* (New York: Council on Economic Priorities, 1983).

12. US Department of Energy, Office of Energy Research, Office of Field Operations Management, *Capsule Review of the DoE Research and Development Field Facilities,* draft copy of the September 1983 edition.

13. Reply to letter by Benjamin Goldman by Ronald W. Cochran, Director, Office of Nuclear Materials Production, US Department of Energy, August 24, 1983.

14. Randall Forsberg, *Call to Halt the Nuclear Arms Race,* Institute for Defense and Disarmament Studies, 1980. Reprinted in Federation of American Scientists, *Seeds of Promise: The First Real Hearings on the Nuclear Freeze* (Andover, MA: Brick House Publishing Co., 1983), appendix.

15. Federation of American Scientists, *Seeds of Promise, op. cit.*

16. *Ibid.*

17. *Long Range Nuclear Weapon Planning Analysis for the Final Report of the DoD/DoE Long Range Resource Planning Group,* Department of Defense/Department of Energy, 1980, Volume one, page 52. Unclassified portions of this report released under the Freedom of Information Act were supplied to CEP by Mike Jendrzejczyk of the Fellowship of Reconciliation.

18. Lawrence Livermore National Laboratory, *Institutional Plan FY 1983–1988,* page 7.

19. Lawrence Livermore National Laboratory, *Institutional Plan FY 1978–1984,* page 2. Reprinted in US House of Representatives, Committee on Science and Technology, *The Role of the National Laboratories in Energy Research and Development* (US GPO: 1977).

20. Calculated by CEP from US Department of Defense, Assistant Secretary of Defense (Comptroller), *Procurement Programs (P-1): The Department of Defense Budget for FY 1984.*

21. Department of Defense, Washington Headquarters Services, *DoD Prime Contract Awards by State, FY 1982* (Washington, DC: DoD 1983).

22. US Department of Commerce, Bureau of Labor Statistics, *Geographic Profile of Employment and Unemployment,* (Washington, DC: US GPO 1983).

23. CEP telephone interview with Rockwell International, El Segundo public relations office, August 7, 1983.

24. Gordon Adams, *The B-1 Bomber: An Analysis of its Strategic Utility, Cost, Constituency, and Economic Impact* (New York: Council on Economic Priorities, 1976), p. 25. The data was originally supplied by Rockwell to Senator George McGovern.

25. *St. Louis Post-Dispatch,* April 21, 1983.

26. Marion Anderson, Jeb Brugmann, and George Erikcek, *Destructive Investment: Nuclear Weapons and Economic Decline* (Lansing: Employment Research Associates, 1983).

27. Congressional Budget Office, *Defense Spending and the Economy,* (Washington: US GPO, 1983), p. 43. For a summary of studies of military spending and employment done in the 1970s, see Michael Edelstein, *The Economic Impact of Military Spending,* (New York: Council on Economic Priorities, 1977). For the most systematic recent analysis of the impact of military spending on employment by industrial sector and occupational category see Robert W. DeGrasse, Jr., *Military Expansion, Economic Decline* (New York: Council on Economic Priorities, 1983).

Table I

Estimated Job Loss as a Result of a Nuclear Freeze
Implemented in Selected Years

	FY 1984	FY 1985	FY 1986	FY 1987	FY 1988
Guided Missile Production[a]	106,407	148,968	155,730	139,205	117,399
Bomber Production[b]	87,080	122,084	140,665	113,455	84,981
Warhead Testing and Production[c]	52,600	52,600	52,600	52,600	52,600
TOTAL	246,087	323,652	348,995	305,260	254,980

a   Projections for guided missile employment are based on outlay projections for the MX, Trident II, Pershing II, and Air-, Sea-, and Ground-Launched Cruise Missiles. The job creation effects for outlays in each year were adjusted for inflation using projections from the Office of the Assistant Secretary of Defense (Comptroller). Since there are no employment projects for Pershing II beyond 1985, the Advanced Cruise Missile program, or the newly proposed "Midgetman" missile program, these features may be understated. However, since guided missile projections for employment per amount of outlays are more accurate than those for the B-1 bomber, which doesn't fit the input-output category of aircraft precisely.

b   Outlays for B-1 were multiplied by input-output employment requirements per $1 billion to arrive at these figures. The figures might be overstated since military aircraft tend to be more capital intensive and use more highly paid design personnel than civilian aircraft. Since outlay projects for the Stealth bomber program are classified, there are no projects for potential employment on that program during the next five years.

c   This figure is only for direct employment of DoE laboratories and production and testing sites primarily engaged in nuclear warhead research, production, and testing. It is an overstatement of the number of direct jobs that would be cut by a Freeze since it includes some research personnel in weapons and energy programs. Cuts in production workers in the warhead complex depend on the details of Freeze implementation (e.g., will one of the plutonium production sites be closed down, how many workers will maintain the component production sites, etc.). Although the direct figure here is overstated, there is *no* estimate for direct effects on employment in supplier industries.

Table II

Employment per $1 Billion Spent, Guided Missile
Production and Other Selected Industries and Services

	Direct Jobs	Total Jobs
Freeze-Related Industries[a]		
Aircraft	13,979	29,100
Radio and Communications Equipment	13,113	28,136
Complete Guided Missiles and Space Vehicles	8,821	20,715
Civilian Industries[b]		
Apparel	25,755	47,453
Iron and Steel Foundries and Forgings	18,860	34,697
Motor Vehicles	9,041	30,394
Petroleum Refining and Related Products	2,718	15,142
Services[c]		
Educational Services	63,130	71,550
Hospitals	42,870	54,267
Local Transit and Intercity Buses	21,550	39,532

NOTE: Jobs per billion dollars are given in 1981 dollars to give a better reflection of the current job creation potential of spending in each of these categories. The input-output model used to determine these figures is based on relationships in the US economy as of 1972, and the employment to output ratios are re-calculated as of 1979. Since specific deflators were used to adjust each category, the ratios among the job creating potentials for each type of spending are slightly different than they would be measured in 1972 dollars, but the ranks among categories have not changed.

Source: *BLS 1979 Employment Requirements Table,* Office of Economic Growth and Employment Projections, US Bureau of Labor Statistics, October 23, 1981.

Continued

a   Complete guided misiles and space vehicles will get the bulk of
    Freeze-related outlays in the coming strategic buildup. Outlays for
    the B-1 bomber will be almost as high in 1986 as the total outlays
    for Freeze-related missiles, but the input-output category for air-
    craft may overstate the actual number of jobs per billion that B-1
    expenditures would crate by a substantial margin due to the focus
    of B-1 expenditures on high cost equipment and engineering talent
    relative to civilian aircraft production. Radio and communications
    is likely to net a substantially smaller sum of Freeze-related outlays
    than the other two categories.

b   Some of these civilian industries, such as motor vehicles, also sup-
    ply some goods to the military, but this is not their major market.

c   Since these figures represent numbers of *jobs*, not numbers of full-
    time equivalent jobs, the ratios between services such as education
    and hospitals which are more likely to use part-time workers and
    the job figures for other categories may be overstated.

Table III

Indirect Employment Generated by a Billion Dollars
of Expenditure in the Guided Missile and Aircraft
Industries

(1972 dollars)

Industry	Indirect Employment	% Total Indirect
COMPLETE GUIDED MISSILES AND SPACE VEHICLES		
Total Employment: 41,638.3		
Direct Employment: 17,729.9		
Indirect Employment: 23,908.4		
Supplier Industries		
Aircraft	3,734.8	15.6%
Eating and Drinking Places	3,253.9	13.6%
Business Services, N.E.C.	1,977.6	8.3%
Radio and Communications Equipment	1,338.2	5.6%
Electronic Components	1,088.2	4.6%
Wholesale Trade	1,043.6	4.4%
Percentage of indirect employment accounted for by top six supplier industries		52.1%

Source: *BLS 1979 Employment Requirements Table,* **Office of Economic Growth Growth and Employment Projection, US Bureau of Labor Statistics, October 23, 1981.**

Continued

Industry	Indirect Employment	% Total Indirect
AIRCRAFT		
Total Employment: 58,941.4		
Direct Employment: 28,098.3		
Indirect Employment: 30,843.1		
Supplier Industries		
Eating and Drinking Places	3,569.1	11.5%
Business Services, N.E.C.	2,101.6	6.8%
Wholesale Trade	1,850.5	6.0%
Hotels and Lodging Places	1,618.2	5.2%
Radio and Communications Equipment	1,492.6	4.8%
Non-Electrical Machinery	1,420.1	4.8%
Electrical Components	1,285.9	4.2%
Professional Services, N.E.C.	967.9	3.1%
Percentage of indirect employment accounted for by top eight supplier industries		46.4%

NOTE: Figures in this table are in 1972 dollars, resulting in much higher jobs per billion totals than those in table II. However, the ranking of supplier industries and the proportion of indirect jobs produced by each remain accurate. The jobs per billion figures are roughly twice as high as they would be in more current year dollars.

Table IV

Manufacturing Impact of MX and Alternatives
Distribution of 'Secondary Impact' Among "Key"
Manufacturing Industries and "Other Manufacturing"
in Percentage Form

	Guided Missile	Mass Transit	Solar[a] Energy	Rail-Roads	Public Utility	Housing
"Key"[b] Manufacturing Industry Impact	14.4%	30.0%	33.9%	46.2%	40.0%	18.0%
Other Manufacturing Impact[c]	45.6%	47.0%	51.1%	27.8%	26.0%	43.0%
Total Manufacturing Impact	60.0%	77.0%	85.0%	74.0%	66.0%	61.0%

a   Peterson, Craig, *"The Solar Energy Industry, An Input-Output Analysis,"* Utah University, 1975. This study consists of creating a column within the 1967 Input Output table (A Matrix) and finding the inverse multipliers for the solar industry (the solar 'column' with the A Matrix) by inversing the 1967 table after including the new or added column for solar. We have used these inverse multipliers despite the fact that they embody the 1967 structure rather than the 1972 structure as used for all other alternatives.

b   "KEY" MANUFACTURING loosely refers to those industries within the manufacturing sector which produce plant and equipment (capital goods) for other industries rather than an 'end product' for final demand (other than for investment final demand). An example would be the metal working equipment industry which produces metal working machines needed by the aircraft and solar development industries, respectively, for jet fighter planes and solar heating collectors.

c   "OTHER" MANUFACTURING would include, for example, the aircraft and solar industries which produce predominantly for final demand rather than for other industries. Their products are 'end products,' such as jet fighter planes or solar collectors. Other examples would be apparel, glass, and cement. While many of these products are produced for industry as well as for final demand, their character is not as directly 'capitalized' as is plant and equipment.

Source: Council on Economic Priorities, *Misguided Expenditure: An Analysis of the MX Missile System.*

Table V

Percentage of Work Force in Each Occupational
Category
(1980)

Occupation	Aircraft & Parts	Communi- cations Equipment	Guided Missiles	Ordnance	Ship Building & Repair	All Mfg.
Professional & Technical	25.4%	32.3%	55.7%	15.2%	7.0%	9.1%
(Engineers)	(11.5%)	(15.0%)	(31.1%)	(5.1%)	(1.8%)	(2.9%)
Managers	7.4%	7.3%	7.2%	5.3%	3.1%	5.9%
Sales	0.8%	0.7%	0.2%	0.4%	0.4%	2.2%
Clerical	13.9%	15.7%	12.3%	10.9%	7.3%	11.3%
Craft	21.3%	12.4%	10.8%	22.5%	40.9%	18.5%
Operatives	27.3%	27.3%	11.2%	33.5%	31.6%	43.4%
Service	2.0%	1.5%	2.1%	5.0%	1.5%	2.0%
Laborers	2.0%	2.9%	0.6%	7.3%	8.3%	7.7%

*Reprinted from *Military Expansion, Economic Decline,* Council on
Economic Priorities.

**Source: US Department of Labor, Bureau of Labor Statistics, "Employ-
ment by Industry and Occupation, 1980 and Projected 1990
Alternatives," unpublished data.**

Table VI

Skills Breakdown of the Workforce at the Department
of Energy's Research and Development Field Facilities

	Total	Scientists and Engineers	Profes- sional and Technical	S & E and P & T as % of Total
DoE Research and Development and Field Facilities	108,997	27,635	37,413	59.6%
Subcategories:				
Multi-program Laboratories	45,707	15,176	17,201	70.8%
Program Dedicated Laboratories	19,162	6,424	7,271	71.5%
Enrichment and Special Nuclear Materials Production	20,604	2,564	6,253	42.3%
Nuclear Warhead Component Fabrication and Assembly	23,560	3,201	7,688	46.2%

NOTE: The DoE figures on R&D field facilities broke down occupational data into five categories: scientists, engineers, other professionals, technicians, and others. We have combined scientists and
engineers and "other professionals" and technicians to come up with
the categories used in this table. The capsule review excludes data on
one key testing site, the Nevada Test Site. This will be discussed
separately.

Source: US Department of Energy, Office of Energy Research, Office of
Field Operations Management, *Capsule Review of the DoE Research and
Development Field Facilities,* Draft of the September 1983 edition.

Table VII

Employment at Nuclear Materials Production and Warhead Component Facilities Affected by a Freeze

Site and Contractor	Description of Nuclear Weapons Role	Total Employees	Employees Affected by a Freeze (and % of Total)
Nuclear Materials Production Facilities			
Savannah River Plant (Dupont), Aiken, SC	Production of plutonium, tritium, and deuterium for use in warheads	10,942	5,732 to 9,803 (52-90%)
Hanford Nuclear Reservation (Rockwell International, United Nuclear), Hanford, WA	Fabrication of fuel for plutonium production reactors, plutonium production, reprocessing of nuclear wastes to recover plutonium	12,715	6,325 (50%)
Idaho National Engineering Labs (EG&G, Exxon), Idaho Falls, ID	Production of highly enriched uranium for nuclear weapons through chemical reprocessing of naval reactor wastes	4,650 to 4,900	558 to 588 (12%)
Feed Materials Production Center (National Lead of Ohio), Fernald, OH	Production of fuel-element cores for plutonium production reactors at Savannah River and Hanford	870	783 (86%)
Extrusion Plant (Reactive Metals, Inc.) Ashtabula, OH	Production of fuel elements for plutonium production reactors at Hanford and Savannah River in cooperation with the Feed Materials Production Center	70	35 (50%)
Subtotal, Nuclear Materials Production		29,256 to 29,497	13,433 to 17,534 (46 to 60%)

Continued

Site and Contractor	Description of Nuclear Weapons Role	Total Employees	Employees Affected by a Freeze (and % of Total)
Fabrication and Assembly of Nuclear Warhead Components			
Oak Ridge Y-12 Plant (Union Carbide) Oak Ridge, TN	Fabrication and certification of nuclear warhead components, development and fabrication of test hardware for the weapons design laboratories	6,800	6,120 (90%)
Kansas City Plant (Bendix Corp.) Kansas City, MO	Production of electrical, electronic, plastic, and mechanical components of nuclear warheads	7,334	6,600 (90%)
Mound Facility (Monsanto) Miamisburg, OH	Production of detonators, explosive timers, and other components of nuclear warheads	2,100	1,890 (90%)
Pinellas Plant (General Electric) Pinellas, FL	Production of neutron generators used in hydrogen bomb triggering mechanisms	1,824	1,642 (90%)
Rocky Flats Plant (Rockwell International) Golden, CO	Production of plutonium triggers for the hydrogen bomb	5,310 to 5,502	4,779 to 4,952 (90%)
Pantex Plant (Mason & Hangar-Silas Mason) Amarillo, TX	Final assembly of all nuclear warheads; retirement of old warheads	2,778	2,500 (90%)
Subtotal, Fabrication and Assembly of Nuclear Warhead Components		26,146 to 26,338	23,531 to 23,704 (90%)

Continued

Site and Contractor	Description of Nuclear Weapons Role	Total Employees	Employees Affected by a Freeze (and % of Total)
Testing Facilities			
Nevada Test Site (Reynolds Electrical and Engineering, EG&G) Nevada	Testing of nuclear weapons	7,500	6,750 (90%)
TOTAL, MATERIALS PRODUCTION, WARHEAD COMPONENT FABRICATION, AND TESTING		62,902 to 63,335	43,714 to 47,988 (69 to 76%)

Source: Department of Energy, Office of Energy Research, Office of Field Operations Management, *Department of Energy Research and Development Field Facilities* (June 1979) and *Capsule Review of DoE Research and Development Field Facilities* (September 1983 advance copy). Total employment figures as of 1983 were received from public affairs officials at each facility.

Table VIII

The Effects of a Nuclear Freeze on Employment at Nuclear Weapons Laboratories

Site and Contractor	Description of Nuclear Weapons Role	No. of Employees Affected by Freeze	Freeze Impact as % of Total Direct Employ- ment on Site
Lawrence Livermore (University of California) Livermore, CA	Nuclear weapons research and design; prototype development and testing	150 to 1,795	4.3 to 52.0%
Los Alamos Scientific Lab (University of California) Los Alamos, NM	Nuclear weapons research and design; prototype development and testing	236 to 1,837	4.4 to 36.0%
Sandia Laboratories (Western Electric Div. of AT&T) Albuquerque, NM	Development of non-nuclear portions of nuclear weapons; engineering development of nuclear warhead designs, testing effects of nuclear explosions and radiation on nuclear warhead performance	650	17.9%
Savannah River Laboratories Aiken, SC	Research and development on production of nuclear materials for warheads, especially plutonium and tritium	348	32.4%
TOTAL		1,384 to 4,630	

Source: The _Institutional Plan_ for each facility, FY 1983-88.

Table IX

Weapons Program RD&T History—Manpower

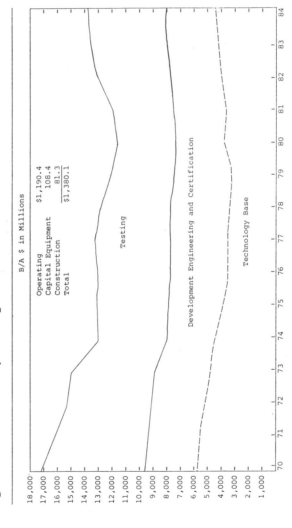

Source: Reprinted from House Armed Services Committee, Subcommittee on Procurement of Military Nuclear Systems, *Hearings on Department of Energy Authorization (National Security Programs) for Fiscal Year 1983.*

Table X

Employment in Guided Missile, Space Vehicle, and
Parts Production, Selected States, 1981

State	State Employment	% National Employment	Guided Missile as % Total State Manufacturing Employment
California	88,685	61.2%	4.3%
Colorado	5,000 to 9,999	3.5 to 6.9%	2.7 to 5.3%
Utah	5,000 to 9,999	3.5 to 6.9%	5.9 to 11.8%
Missouri	2,500 to 4,999	1.7 to 3.5%	0.6 to 1.1%
Arizona	2,500 to 4,999	1.7 to 3.5%	1.6 to 3.2%
Massachusetts	1,000 to 2,499	0.7 to 1.7%	0.1 to 0.4%
Washington	500 to 999	0.3 to 0.7%	0.2 to 0.3%
TOTAL	105,195 to 122,189	72.7 to 84.4%	

Source: US Department of Commerce, Bureau of the Census, *County Business Patterns, 1981,* for the selected states and the U.S.

Table XI

States Receiving the Largest Dollar Amounts of Prime Contract Awards for Guided Missiles Affected by the Freeze, FY 1982 (Millions of Dollars)

State	System and % of Total Awards for That System				Total Awards for Freeze Related Missiles
	MX	Trident	Cruise Missiles	Pershing II	
California	$ 685.2 (39.71%)	$ 896.7 (77.27%)	$ 449.1 (35.99%)	--	$2,031.0
Colorado	452.3 (26.21%)	--	--	--	452.3
Florida	37.0 (2.14%)	9.1 (0.79%)	--	$351.9 (88.30%)	398.0
Massachu-setts	225.4 (13.06%)	155.8 (13.42%)	--	14.0 (3.51%)	395.2
Missouri	--	--	224.5 (17.98%)	--	224.6
Washington	77.0 (4.46%)	--	109.8 (8.79%)	--	186.8
Utah	179.6 (10.40%)	--	--	--	179.6
Michigan	--	--	165.0 (13.20%)	--	165.0
Maryland	--	16.3 (1.20%)	89.1 (7.13%)	--	105.4
Kansas	--	--	83.5 (6.68%)	--	83.5
TOTAL	$1,656.5 (95.98%)	$1,077.9 (92.68%)	$1,121.1 (89.75%)	$365.9 (91.81%)	$4,221.4

Source: Department of Defense, Washington Headquarters Services, "Alphabetic Detail of DoD Prime Contract Awards Above $10,000, FY 1982."

Table XII

Employment Effects of Altenative Expenditures As
Compared to B-1 Generated Employment

	Difference in Number of Persons Employed as Compared to B-1		
	1976	1977	1980
Tax Cut	+10,000	+10,000	+30,000
Housing	+20,000	+30,000	+70,000
Welfare-Public Works	+20,000	+20,000	+60,000

Source Drawn from Chase Econometrics Associates, Economic Impact of the B-1 Program on the U.S. Economy, Table 14, T2.

III

Opportunity Costs of The Nuclear Weapons Buildup

Significant amounts of employment and income are undoubtedly produced by spending over $20 billion per year purchasing nuclear weapons systems.(1) To obtain a realistic picture of the impact of these expenditures, it is necessary to measure their "opportunity costs": what would be the economic effects of using these funds for other purposes? CEP has assessed the economic effects of three alternative uses of the funds currently committed to nuclear weapons production: 1) restoration of basic human services programs; 2) public investments in housing, mass transit, infrastructure, and employment and training programs; and 3) cutting the Federal deficit by an amount equal to budget savings from a nuclear Freeze. The analysis focuses on concrete opportunities that have substantial support from community and human service organizations, state and local government officials, trade unions, and the business community. Applying Freeze savings to these options can make a significant contribution in addressing some of the major economic problems in the United States today.

Before presenting specific opportunities offered by a Freeze, we will review the consequences of the Reagan Administration's military buildup.

Opportunity Costs in Practice: The Reagan Administration's Shift of Funding from Service Programs to Weapons Programs

"Mr. Weinberger contended, as he has in the past, that defense budget cuts can't significantly shrink the deficit. He contended that each defense dollar generates 50 cents in revenue, and that a $10

Reagan Administration officials consistently cite the economic *benefits* of the current military buildup. They rarely cite the *costs* in jobs and services that result from the parallel cuts in civilian programs. In fact, from 1981 through 1983, military spending increases were matched almost dollar for dollar by cuts in civilian service and investment programs. This dramatic shift from civilian to military programs is a clear example of 'opportunity costs' in practice. While procurement and research and development spending on new weapons has been the fastest growing category within the military buildup, programs aimed at poor households have borne the brunt of the civilian cuts. According to the Congressional Budget Office, the largest percentage cuts in program funding have been in programs such as public service employment, community services, compensatory education, child nutrition, and Food Stamps. These programs are specifically targeted toward low income households.(2) Forty percent of the benefit reductions to individuals since 1981 have been from households with incomes of less than $10,000. The average benefit reduction for these households was $430 each, roughly three times the average reduction for households with incomes above $20,000.(3)

The economic effects of increased military spending go beyond the effects of budgetary tradeoffs. CEP's *Military Expansion, Economic Decline* demonstrates that high military spending is closely linked to lower levels of investment and productivity growth. Both of these, in turn, contribute to slower rates of overall economic growth.(4) The study surveys data on military spending and economic performance in 17 advanced industrial nations covering two decades. It finds that the United States has the highest levels of military spending and the *lowest* levels of investment and productivity growth during this period. High levels of military spending have a stronger correlation with slower investment and productivity growth than the level of industrial maturity of a nation, a commonly cited explanation for declining US economic performance. Two other factors commonly blamed for US economic problems, high civilian government spending and labor costs, showed no correlation at all with the slowdown in the US economy.(5)

The macroeconomic analysis carried out in *Military Expansion, Economic Decline* cannot be applied to nuclear weapons spending alone because of the relatively small percentage of US military expenditures (20 to 25 percent) devoted to this purpose and the small number of countries producing nuclear weapons. For this reason, the focus of most of the analysis of this chapter is devoted to concrete and immediate opportunity costs of nuclear weapons spending.

Restoring Basic Services

Budget savings from a Freeze could be used to restore basic services such as nutrition and income maintenance programs to families and individuals most in need. Cuts in these services have been opposed vigorously by the National Conference of Mayors and nationwide advocacy groups such as the Children's Defense Fund.(6) Freeze savings could also be applied to education, day care, and health and safety programs offering future employment opportunities and improved quality of work life for low and middle income households.

All cuts in Aid for Families with Dependent Children, Food Stamps, child nutrition programs, Federal aid to education, day care, and the Occupational Safety and Health Administration could be restored to their 1981 levels using budget savings from a nuclear Freeze. The five year Freeze savings would not only restore programs for 1984, but could maintain all of these programs at 1981 levels for the next five years *without any other changes* in Reagan Administration tax or budget projections. This represents a conservative estimate of what these savings could do. They could potentially be used to expand these programs beyond their 1981 levels of service and resources. Table I describes the impact of recent cuts and the costs of restoring each of these programs.

Table I shows how far $81 billion of the $92 billion in budget outlay savings could go toward restoring needed services. It would be enough to restore Food Stamp benefits to one million people and AFDC benefits to 350,000 families. All education program cuts could be restored, and all new proposed cuts offset. Day care and a wide range of social and community service programs could be restored and maintained at 1981 levels. And recent and proposed cuts in the Occupational Safety and Health Administration could be offset. With all this, $11 billion in outlay savings is still available and could be applied to readjustment and re-training assistance and community planning grants for workers and areas most affected by a nuclear Freeze. This would provide $20,000 in re-training and readjustment benefits per affected worker if the maximum 350,000 workers were displaced, plus $4 billion for administration and local planning. This compares favorably with provisions in the most comprehensive economic conversion bills discussed in Congress.(7)

The services discussed here are either transfer payments (AFDC and Food Stamps), investments in development of the capabilities of future members of the work force (education), or contributions to the quality of work life and potential for full participation in the work force (OSHA and day care). They do not entail major new investments in buildings or equipment, and would have little direct impact on the manufacturing and technical fields suffering displacement under a Freeze. The majority of jobs created would be in teaching and related educational job categories and the affected human services agencies. These programs essentially would benefit a different group of workers and communities than those that would be affected by a Freeze. For this reason, the provision of planning funds and income support to those displaced by a Freeze would be an important complement.

Public Investments

Funding public investments in relatively large scale projects in housing, mass transit, and infrastructure which might not otherwise be undertaken is another alternative. Investment in publicly supported jobs programs, drastically reduced under the Reagan Administration, is also an option.

Key programs in housing, mass transit, and public employment have been cut even more substantially than major service programs. Funding for public housing and Section 8 subsidized housing for low income people was reduced by more than 60 percent between FY 1981 and FY 1984, from more than $35 billion to less than $13 billion.(8) The Comprehensive Employment and Training Act was cut from $7.5 billion to $3.1 billion from 1981 to 1982, and its public service employment provisions have been completely eliminated.(9) Federal aid to mass transit programs has decreased in dollar terms from $4.9 to $4.3 billion from FY 1981 to FY 1984.(10)

Aid to public transportation, ranging from subways in large urban areas to bus service for suburban and rural areas, receives a relatively modest level of Federal support. This continues despite the environmental benefits and energy savings implied in decreasing dependence on the automobile as a major means of transport. As of 1980, nearly two-thirds of all work trips were made by cars carrying one individual.(11) Reductions in operating subsidies for mass transit have come at a time when most large cities are faced with declining local sources of revenue to offset cuts in Federal support. The production and engineering skills needed to support a Federal mass transit program could draw on the same pool of skills currently engaged in nuclear weapons development, testing, and production. However, a mass transit program of the size posited here would not create the same number of jobs, nor would it need as high a proportion of scientists and engineers within its work force.

Public Works, Public Employment, and Housing Construction

The AFL-CIO's "Economic Program for Jobs and Fairness" consists of public works, housing construction, public employment, service restoration, and emergency income assistance for the unemployed. The public works and public employment sections of the program would cost a total of $46 billion for FY 1984 or over three times the $13.7 billion in budget outlays a Freeze would produce in this fiscal year. Table II gives details on the cost and employment effects of each major component of the program. Freeze savings for FY 1984 would be sufficient to cover the proposals for youth programs, along with the housing or accelerated public works programs. Total job creation would be 500,000 to 750,000. Either combination would include part-time employment, temporary construction jobs, and full-time employment. Even so, the proposals compare quite favorably with the less than 250,000 jobs in guided missile, bomber, and warhead production that would be eliminated by a Freeze implemented in FY 1984.

The accelerated public works investment includes funds for a combination of hospitals, schools, solid waste and water treatment plants, highways, bridges, port facilities, and urban mass transit projects. The housing program supports *new construction* of 170,000 units per year.(12) Youth employment projects include an expanded Job Corps, establishment of a youth conservation corps, and other special training and employment projects aimed at jobless teenagers. Each of these areas of investment are targeted to sectors of industry (construction), areas of need (housing), and groups of the population (unemployed youth) that have suffered more than their share of the nation's recent economic difficulties. This is in sharp contrast with nuclear weapons spending that stimulates specialized, well paid job categories in science and engineering, and creates relatively few jobs for production workers.

Reducing Federal Deficits

If the Freeze savings were applied toward cutting Federal budget deficits, only modest relief from the $150 to $200 billion yearly Federal budget deficits predicted by the Reagan Administration from now through 1987 would be accomplished.(13) Freeze cuts would, however, meet the important criteria of those in business and government concerned about Federal domination of credit sources during a period of economic recovery. Freeze related savings would be greatest in the 'outyears' of 1985 and 1986. The financial community is most concerned about Federal borrowing 'crowding out' investors and consumers during this time period. Secretary of Defense Weinberger testified before Congress that cuts in weapons systems offer little help with budget deficits because so little of the money authorized is spent in the year of the authorization. This same factor, however, means that by 1985 and 1986, authorizations from previous years will have resulted in high levels of outlay savings on strategic weapons systems.

The contribution of military spending to record government deficits has not been completely ignored within the Reagan Administration. In a November 1983 speech to the Southern Economic Association, chairman of the Council on Economic Advisors Martin Feldstein presented a statistical analysis showing that the enormous growth in actual and projected federal deficits between 1980 and 1988 is principally tied to growth in military spending. He asserted that Social Security and Medicare "will have no net effect" on the deficit, while other civilian programs would contribute to a net reduction of the deficit during this period. Feldstein concluded that if more wasn't done to cut deficits in 1986 and beyond, "I'm worried about the risks to which we're exposing the economy."(14) The Bipartisan Budget Appeal organized by six former US Secretaries of the Treasury, has gone a step further by arguing that projected deficits for the coming period "threaten to lock the economy in stagnation for the remainder of this century."(15) This group's proposal for cutting the 1985 deficit to $75 billion from its original projection of $250 billion, includes $25 billion in defense budget cuts along with a series of further civilian cuts and tax increases. This suggestion compares favorably with projected Freeze savings for FY 1985, as indicated in Table III.

According to the Congressional Budget Office, continuing high deficits at the levels built-in to current spending plans could "increase the risk of aborting economic recovery."(16) Many economists from government and the financial community agree. There is disagreement about specific effects a given level of reduction in deficits might have on the economy. Both Paul Volcker, Chairman of the Federal Reserve Bank, and Martin Feldstein, Chairman of President Reagan's Council of Economic Advisors, argue that Federal deficits of $200 to $300 billion

48

per year after 1985 would hold back "the growth of interest sensitive sectors of the economy such as autos, plant and equipment, housing and exports."(17) The National Association of Realtors, representing 700,000 realtors across the country, argues that cutting the deficit by $100 billion could substantially reduce interest rates to a level where housing starts could triple and overall employment increase by 800,000 within a two year period.(18)

The Diversion of Scientists and Engineers into Nuclear Weapons Programs

Taking the focus off alternative uses of the *funds* from a nuclear Freeze, what are the opportunity costs of a nuclear weapons buildup based on the *types of resources* devoted to it? Spending on nuclear warheads and nuclear delivery vehicles (discussed in chapter II) places a heavy reliance on technical personnel. Are the numbers of scientists and engineers engaged in nuclear weapons systems research, development, and production so large a proportion of the total pool as to undermine the pursuit of solutions to key civilian research and development problems?

As CEP documented in *Military Expansion, Economic Decline,* Pentagon funding of research and development projects in recent years has pushed technology into increasingly esoteric (and expensive) directions. Despite early development of semiconductors under DoD auspices, most of the commercial uses of this technology, in everything from consumer electronics to industrial robots, have been developed most successfully by Japanese firms. These firms receive less government military funding and more support for projects aimed at commercial application of new technologies than US firms. The Department of Defense's Very High Speed Integrated Circuit program (VHSIC) carries on this trend in its attempt to encourage US semiconductor firms to focus on the development of computer chips with ten times the density and 100 times the speed of current models. Their use—everything from night vision devices to Intercontinental Ballistic Missiles.(19) As for civilian uses, one electronics industry executive asserts that "those incredibly complex VHSI circuits that the military wants don't seem to have their use elsewhere."(20)

Is research and development spending on nuclear weapons systems substantial enough to be considered a major contributing factor to the distortion of US technological development? In FY 1984, *one-third* of total U.S. military R&D went for work on strategic delivery vehicles and nuclear warheads, according to a CEP analysis of National Science Foundation data. (21) Research and development funding in these areas has grown twice as fast as overall military R&D since 1981. Nuclear weapons systems, therefore, take up a substantially higher share of R&D funding than of overall military spending. In what may be the most extreme example of this tendency, the MX missile has consumed over $6 billion in R&D funding for a program that may result in the production of as few as 100 missiles if current plans hold.(22) The US has consistently devoted over six times as much of its (much larger) GNP to military R&D as its major industrial competitors West Germany and Japan. In fact, it appears that the US devotes more funding to *nuclear weapons* R&D than these other nations do to *total* military R&D.(23)

No systematic survey of the proportion of US scientists and engineers engaged primarily in work on nuclear weapons systems has been done. However, surveys by the National Science Foundation indicate that a minimum of 15 to 25 percent of the nation's scientists and engineers are primarily involved in projects funded by the Pentagon.(24) Given that at least one-third of military R&D spending in the US is currently applied to strategic forces and nuclear warheads, CEP estimates that between five and eight percent of the nation's scientists and engineers are involved in nuclear weapons systems work.(25)

Between one in twelve and one in twenty of the nation's scientists and engineers are involved in nuclear weapons related work. This is probably conservative, but it is the best available estimate short of a systematic survey. Although a minority of the country's scientists and engineers are involved in nuclear weapons work, their numbers become substantial when considering the need for work in environmental, energy, and civilian technological problems. One important example of missed opportunities is the distortion of research priorities within the US Department of Energy which has developed as a consequence of its responsibility for research, development, and fabrication of nuclear warheads.

Reagan's DoE: The Squeeze on Non-nuclear Energy Programs

"I want to make clear that I consider the Department's defense responsibilities to be the most important that we have. This is not simply because the budget for these defense activities is the largest segment of the

total DoE budget; rather, it is because the nuclear weapons the Department develops and manufactures and the role the Department plays in the continuing improvement and support of the nuclear Navy are so very crucial to our national defense posture."

Secretary of Energy Donald Hodel, Testimony before the House Armed Services Committee, March 1, 1983

The Department of Energy is unique among Federal agencies. It carries out civilian functions of energy research and development alongside the military function of research, development, testing, and production of all US nuclear bombs. In recent years, the agency's military functions have received priority: while the overall DoE budget has dropped 8 percent in dollar terms from FY 1981 through 1984, energy research and development programs have been cut 39 percent (26). Non-nuclear energy programs have been hardest hit: solar and other renewables, conservation, and fossil energy programs have each been cut over 60 percent during the last three years. Part of the impetus for cuts in non-nuclear energy research and development comes from the Reagan Administration's policy of "maximum reliance on the private sector" in solving energy problems. Two other important factors behind these budget cuts are directly tied to DoE's military responsibilities.(27)

The first is the growing share of overall departmental funds consumed by Atomic Energy Defense Activities: from 1981 to 1984 these military programs grew from 30 percent of total DoE budget authority to 53 percent.(28)

The second factor behind the decline in alternative and fossil energy R&D is tied to the history and institutional mandate of the agency's eight multi-program laboratories. Each of these facilities were developed as part of the plans for the Manhattan project—the project responsible for building the atomic bombs used against Hiroshima and Nagasaki.(29) These large and well-equipped laboratories, employing 2/3 of the personnel at DoE R&D facilities, were not allowed by law to do non-nuclear energy R&D until 1971.(30) Even today, the three largest multi-program laboratories, Los Alamos, Lawrence Livermore, and Sandia, have a set of criteria for accepting new projects that favors nuclear projects over alternative energy projects. These criteria were aptly summarized in the 1983 *Institutional Plan* of Lawrence Livermore Laboratory:

> Our primary role is to perform the research, development, and testing associated with the nuclear design aspects of all phases of the nuclear weapon life cycle, and perform associated national security related tasks.
> We have a corollary role to address other important national problems meeting the following criteria: *synergism with our weapons program;* suffi-

cient size, importance and complexity to make effective use of significant or unique laboratory capabilities; and relative distinction from the research interests of the university and industrial sectors.(31)

Requiring energy projects to complement the weapons work of the largest multi-program laboratories of the DoE led to neglect of non-nuclear energy programs even during the years when non-nuclear programs were better funded. A 1978 General Accounting Office study of the eight multi-program laboratories determined that "the nonnuclear energy tasks undertaken by the eight laboratories have been relatively small and often appear to focus on fragmented portions of technologies."(32) A Freeze on warhead production could potentially allow for a more systematic and intensive approach to alternative energy programs within the DoE's research complex.

Conclusion

The $98 billion in potential budget savings from a Freeze over the next five years is a relatively small sum compared with either the overall military buildup or the cost of meeting basic needs for employment, housing, food, health care, and environmental quality in the United States. Nevertheless, these funds could make a significant contribution toward solving specific problems:

- Applied to services, Freeze savings could restore all cuts in Aid to Families with Dependent Children, Food Stamps, child nutrition, Federal education programs, Social and Community Services Block Grants, and the Occupational Safety and Health Administration. These programs, serving tens of millions of Americans, could be restored to 1981 level funding and maintained against inflation *for the next five years* without adding to Federal government deficits.

- Applied to public investment and public employment programs, FY 1984 Freeze savings alone could support construction of 170,000 housing units, and a jobs program for 430,000 unemployed teenagers.

- Applied to cutting federal deficits, Freeze savings could reduce the Federal government's projected deficit by 13 to 21 billion dollars per year in each of the next five years, a percentage reduction of 7 to 12 percent each year.

The greatest economic opportunities offered by a Freeze would come later if a Freeze agreement held and the $425 billion in nuclear weapons programs funding planned through the end of this century could be devoted to other purposes.

Footnotes

1. The $20 billion figure represents the amount spent on procurement and R&D for nuclear warheads and delivery vehicles, not the total costs of nuclear forces. Estimates of the full costs of researching, producing, deploying and maintaining US nuclear forces are discussed in chapter II of this report.

2. Congressional Budget Office, *Major Legislative Changes in Human Resource Programs Since January 1981,* (Washington: CBO August 1983), pp. 14-23.

3. *Ibid.,* p. 79.

4. Robert W. DeGrasse, Jr., *Military Expansion, Economic Decline,* (New York: Council on Economic Priorities, 1983), chapter 2.

5. *Ibid.,* ch. 2.

6. See Robert Pear, "Reagan Hunger Call", *New York Times,* August 5, 1983, which cites Mayor Ernest N. Dutch Morial's call for an "omnibus anti-hunger bill" on behalf of the US Conference of Mayors; Children's Defense Fund, *A Children's Defense Budget* (Washington: CDF, 1983), which presents the details of that organization's proposed "Children's Survival Bill".

7. See chapter V, footnote 12 for a discussion of the re-training and readjustment provisions of Rep. Ted Weiss's HR 425, "The Defense Economic Adjustment Act", with an estimate of the short-term funding it would provide.

8. Cushing Dolbeare, "Low Income Housing Assistance", in Children's Defense Fund, *A Children's Defense Budget,* op. cit. Figures cover FY 1984 Reagan Administration proposals.

9. Jobs Roundtable, "Employment and Training Programs", in Fair Budget Action Campaign, *An Organizer's Manual* (Washington: FBAC 1983).

10. US Office of Management and Budget, *The Budget of the United States Government,* (Washington: US GPO), Fiscal Year 1985 and 1982 editions.

11. Congressional Budget Office, *Public Works Infrastructure: Policy Considerations for the 1980s* (Washington: CBO 1983), p. 37.

12. "AFL-CIO Economic Program for Jobs and Fairness", The AFL-CIO *Federationist,* March 19, 1983. For further background on this proposal see the testimony of Lane Kirkland, President, AFL-CIO, before the House Budget Committee, *Budget and Fiscal Policy for 1984,* vol. 3, (Washington: US GPO 1983).

13. See table III, this chapter for Reagan Administration and Congressional Budget Office projections of Federal budget deficits over the next five years.

14. *Wall Street Journal,* November 22, 1983.

15. *New York Times,* January 20, 1983.

16. Congressional Budget Office, *Reducing the Federal Deficit: Spending and Revenue Options,* (Washington: US GPO 1983).

17. *New York times,* January 21, 1983.

18. Testimony of Jack Carlson, National Association of Realtors, before the Committee on the Budget, US House of Representatives, in *Budget Issues for Fiscal year 1983,* volume 5, (Washington: US GPO 1982). For further details on the methodology used to make these projections see National Association of Realtors, *The Realtors Economic Package* (Washington, National Association of Realtors, 1983).

19. DeGrasse, *op. cit.,* chapter 3.

20. Mary Kaldor, *The Baroque Arsenal* (New York: Hill and Wang, 1981), p. 94.

21. National Science Foundation, Division of Science Resources Studies, *Federal R&D Funding by Budget Function, Fiscal Years 1982–84* (Washington: NSF April 1983).

22. US Department of Defense, *Program Acquisition Costs by Weapon System,* Fiscal Year 1980, 1981, 1982, 1983, and 1984 editions.

23. According to an average calculated from National Science Board, *Science Indicators 1978* (Washington: US GPO 1979), in Robert DeGrasse, Paul Murphy, and William Ragen, *The Costs and Consequences of Reagan's Military Buildup* (New York: Council on Economic Priorities, 1982), p. 23. The calculation showed that from 1960 through 1976, US military R&D expenditures averaged over 1.2% of GNP, while West Germany devoted .2% of GNP to military R&D and Japan devoted less than .05% of its GNP to military R&D over the period. Since in recent years nuclear weapons related R&D has accounted for 1/3 of total US military R&D, it is safe to assume that US funding of nuclear weapons related R&D is higher both in absolute currency terms and as a percentage of GNP than the *total* military R&D expenditures of countries like Japan and West Germany.

24. This estimate was made in Robert DeGrasse, et. al., *Military Expansion, Economic Decline,* op. cit., p. 102. It was based on a series of sources, the most systematic of which were Richard Dempsey and Douglas Schmude, "Occupational Impact of Defense Expenditures", *Monthly Labor Review,* December 1971, p. 12, and National Science Foundation, *Characteristics of Experienced Scientists and Engineers 1978,* (Washington, D.C.: NSF 1979). The estimate of 15 to 25 percent of scientists and engineers primarily involved in projects for the Pentagon is for the 1970s, and DeGrasse notes that "this percentage is likely to rise significantly during the 1980s. As a result, our estimate of 5 to 8 percent of scientists and engineers involved in work on nuclear weapons and their delivery vehicles should be viewed as a minimum estimate.

25. The share of funding for nuclear weapons in total military R&D does not offer a precise indication of the proportion of Pentagon supported scientists and engineers involved in military work. Some scientists and engineers are engaged in the *production* of weapons as well. However, since the sectors most involved in nuclear weapons production (aircraft, guided missiles, and nuclear warheads) have higher proportions of technical personnel than other weapons production sectors such as ordnance and shipbuilding, there is no reason to believe that allowing for the numbers of scientists and engineers in weapons production would reduce our estimate of the proportion of Pentagon supported scientists and engineers involved in nuclear weapons related work. See chapter II of this report for further background on the heavy concentration of scientific and engineering personnel in aircraft, guided missile, and warhead production.

26. Calculated from US Department of Energy, *Budget Highlights,* (Washington, DC: US DOE), Fiscal Year 1985 and 1982 editions.

27. For a review of the Reagan Administration position on government involvement in energy development, see US Department of Energy, *The National Energy Policy Plan,* (Washington: US GPO 1983), p. 1-2.

28. See note 26.

29. Comptroller General of the United States, Report to the Congress, *The Multi-program Laboratories: A National Resource for Nonnuclear Energy Research, Development, and Demonstration* (Washington: US GPO, 1978). Argonne National Laboratories, which specializes in nuclear energy research, wasn't built until after World War II, but its construction was planned by the Manhattan Engineering District, US Army, which directed the development of atomic weapons during World War II.

30. Comptroller General, *The Multi-Program Laboratories,* op. cit.

31. Lawrence Livermore National Laboratory, *Institutional Plan FY 83-88* (Livermore, CA: LLNL 1982), p. 4.

32. Comptroller General, *op. cit.*

Table I

The Cost of Restoring Major Cuts in Human Services, Education, and Health and Safety Programs

FY 1984-1988 ($bn)

Program	Impact of Budget Cuts	Cost of Restoring 1981 Level Funding, and Avoiding Further Proposed Cuts, FY 1984-88
Income Support		
Aid to Families with Dependent Children	$2.1 billion in cuts have resulted in 350,000 families losing all benefits, and substantial benefit reductions for 300,000 more families.	$ 9.742 billion
Nutrition		
Food Stamps	$2.9 billion in budget cuts, resulting in one million people losing Food Stamps, with reductions in benefits for the majority of the 21 million people still in the program.	16.393 billion
Child Nutrition	$2.3 billion in cuts have eliminated free or subsidized school lunches for 3 million children, school breakfasts for 900,000 children, and summer school lunches for 500,000 children.	9.731 billion
Education		
All Programs	Cost of maintaining 1981 level funding and avoiding further proposed cuts.	36.095 billion
Compensatory Education (Chapter I of the Education Consolidation and Improvement Act)	$1.1 billion in cuts in this program for remedial and compensatory mathematics and reading instruction for educationally disadvantaged children living in low income areas have been enacted.	4.700 billion

Continued

Program	Impact of Budget Cuts	Cost of Restoring 1981 Level Funding, and Avoiding Further Proposed Cuts, FY 1984-88
Education (cont'd)		
Education for Handicapped Children (Education for All Handicapped Children Act, P.L. 94-142)	FY 1984 proposals are $0.368 billion lower than FY 1980 level funding. Federal support for this program serving 4 million handicapped children nationwide has dropped from 12% of total funding in 1980 to 9.4% in 1983.	0.910 billion
Education Block Grants (Chapter II of the Education Consolidation and Improvement Act)	FY 1984 proposal is $0.556 billion less than 1980 levels for this program covering funding for 30 former educational grant programs including Emergency School Aid to districts implementing desegregation plans. Overall funding of these programs is now less than one half 1980 levels.	$ 1.562 billion
Bilingual Education	Reduced to nearly one third of 1980 level funding, in a program currently serving less than 10% of potentially eligible students.	0.504 billion
Impact Aid (School Aid to Federally Affected Areas)	The number of local school districts receiving aid to help cover the costs of educating children of employees at major federal facilities has dropped from 4,300 in 1979 to 2,000 in 1983.	2.574 billion
Vocational Education	Federal funding for vocational education programs, accounting for 10% of all vocational education spending and over half of all spending for vocational education targeted to disadvantaged students, has been cut by 12% in two years.	1.903 billion
Aid to Higher Education (Including Pell Grants, Guaranteed Student Loans, and Other Student Financial Assistance)	Over 700,000 fewer students received guaranteed student loans, and an estimated 400,000 fewer students received Pell grants for low income applicants to college programs as a result of 1981 through 1983 federal budget cuts.	8.581 billion
Other Education Programs		15.341 billion

Continued

Other Services

Social Services Block Grant	Funding for a whole range of social services including day care, foster care, homemaker services, meals and transportation for senior citizens, and family planning were combined in this block grant and cut 21% across the board.	$ 4.173 billion
Community Services Block Grant	This block grant, replacing programs formerly run by the Community Services Administration and targeted to low income (mostly urban) areas, has been cut by over one third, and proposed for elimination as of 1984.	1.477 billion
Cost of Avoiding Proposed Community and Social Services Cuts	The Reagan Administration has proposed an additional total of $2.9 billion in cuts for social and community services for FY 1984 through 1988.	2.900 billion
Occupational Safety and Health Administration	Funds have been cut by 10% since 1980, resulting in a reduction in compliance officers from 1,683 to 1,000, a 45% reduction in workplace inspections, and a 200% increase in the backlog of uninvestigated employee complaints.	0.198 billion
	Total cost of restoration and avoiding further cuts, all programs, 1984-88	$80.709 billion

Sources: 1981 through 1983 cuts and their impacts, Congressional Budget Office, *Major Legislative Changes in Human Resources Programs Since January 1981*, August 1983; Children's Defense Fund, *A Children's Defense Budget: An Analysis of the President's FY 1984 Budget and Children*; Office of Management and Budget, *Budget of the United States Government Fiscal Year 1984*; National Education Association, "Testimony of the National Education Association on Education Appropriations for Fiscal Year 1984 before the Subcommittee on Labor/HHS/Education, Committee on Appropriations, US Senate", May 3, 1983; and The Fair Budget Action Coalition, *An Organizer's Manual*, 1983 (for information on proposed further cuts: Congressional Budget Office, *An Analysis of the President's Budgetary Proposals for Fiscal Year 1984*, February 1983. This publication was also used as the basis for estimates of the costs of maintaining programs at inflation adjusted levels for FY 1984 through 1988.

Table II

AFL-CIO Program for "Jobs and Fairness"

Programs	Increased Budget Outlays ($ billion)		Direct Jobs (thousands)	
	Supplement to FY 1983	1984	1983	1984
Community Development Supplemental Jobs	$ 5.0	$10.0	420	835
Youth Programs	1.5	3.0	215	430
Displaced Worker Program	1.0	2.0	--	--
Accelerated Public Works	5.0	10.0	170	340
Extended Unemployment Insurance	2.0	6.0	--	--
Housing	5.0	10.0	85	180
Health Care for the Unemployed	3.0	5.0	--	--
TOTAL	$22.5	· $46.0	880	1,785

Source: "AFL-CIO Economic Program for Jobs and Fairness," The AFL-CIO *Federationist*, 3/19/83. For full details of the AFL-CIO program, see this edition of the *Federationist*.

Table III

Projected Budget Deficits With and Without A Nuclear Freeze

FY 1984-1988 ($bn)

	FY 1984	FY 1985	FY 1986	FY 1987	FY 1988
Original Projection of Deficits					
OMB[a]	$183.7	$180.4	$177.1	$180.5	$152.0
(CBO)[b]	($190)	($190)	($203)	($220)	($232)
Freeze Savings (Outlays)	$13.7	$19.2	$21.5	$20.2	$17.8
Deficits with a Freeze[c]					
OMB	$170.0	$161.2	$155.6	$160.3	$134.2
(CBO)	($176.3)	($170.8)	($181.5)	($199.8)	($214.2)
% Decrease in Deficit Under a Freeze					
OMB	7.5%	10.6%	12.1%	11.2%	11.7%
(CBO)	(7.2%)	(10.1%)	(10.6%)	(9.2%)	(7.7%)

Notes:

a   These deficit figures are from Office of Management and Budget, *Budget of the United States Government, FY 1985*. They are based on projections from the President's Fiscal Year 1985 budget proposal.

b   These deficit figures are Congressional Budget Office baseline estimates as of February 1984. These baseline estimates reflect maintenance of existing spending commitments (i.e., no allowance is made for either real growth or further cuts beyond what is already passed into law).

c   Freeze savings figures combine estimates on outlay savings for delivery vehicles (chapter II, table I) and warhead production (chapter II, table II).

Continued

Note On Data: These are the best projections on federal deficits available as this study goes to press. Actual deficits incurred inevitably vary considerably from five year projections because of imperfect forecasting of economic conditions and changes in planned Federal or Congressional action. We have assumed that all Freeze savings become budget savings. The actual situation will be more complex, including offsetting expenditures for unemployment compensation for displaced workers, contract cancellation payments to contractors, and other related economic changes. However, since data was not available to measure these effects precisely, the assumption that all Freeze related spending cuts become net budget outlay savings was adopted. Given that the savings figures are conservative (excluding estimates for the Advanced Cruise Missile, Stealth bomber, and Midgetman missile, and making no allowance for cost overruns on the systems included), the exclusion of offsetting factors from consideration may be mitigated.

IV

The Corporate Role in Nuclear Weapons Production

Nuclear weapons production is a multi-billion dollar business. The largest contracts are awarded to the major producers of the B-1 bomber, MX missile, Trident I and II missiles, the Air-, Sea-, and Ground-Launched Cruise Missiles, and the Pershing II missile. These firms, while accounting for over half of the prime and subcontract awards for work on nuclear systems, represent a small fraction of the more than 10,000 companies engaged in some aspect of nuclear weapons production. This figure does not include over 500 suppliers who provide components to the nine largest DoE warhead research and production laboratories.(1)

The B-1 Bomber

The Reagan Administration announced its decision to build 100 B-1B bombers as part of its "strategic modernization program." This decision marked a reversal of the Carter Administration's 1977 cancellation of the B-1 program on the grounds that the development of the Air-Launched Cruise Missile, capable of penetrating Soviet air defenses, made the development of the bomber redundant.(2)

Current plans call for the full complement of 100 B-1Bs to be deployed by 1988. Its role as a strategic bomber, capable of getting through Soviet air defense systems, is designated to last only until the early 1990s. At that time, it will be replaced by the Advanced Technology or "Stealth" bomber. The "Stealth" bomber program is classified, but reports in the aerospace press and from the Pentagon indicate that 100 to 165 of the planes may be built, at a cost of $36 to $40 billion.(3)

The four associate prime contractors for the B-1B bomber are Rockwell International (airframe and final assembly); General Electric (engine); Boeing (offensive avionics system); and Eaton AIL Division (defensive avionics system). Table I summarizes the contract awards to each company, and the principal locations of work.

The total B-1B program is estimated to cost a minimum of $39.8 billion. Since Fiscal Year 1982 was only the first full year of awards for the B-1B, revenues to the major contractors for B-1B work will expand dramatically in the years to come. Eaton estimates that its total awards for the program will exceed $1 billion, more than five times its FY 1982 total. The Department of Defense has announced an additional commitment of $2.6 billion to Rockwell since the end of FY 1982 for multi-year procurement funding of the first 92 B-1Bs, advance purchases of parts for the first 46 aircraft, and full scale production of the first seven aircraft.(4) Although not all of these funds have been forwarded to the company yet, they indicate the scope of Rockwell's revenues from the program in the coming period.

The MX ICBM

The MX Intercontinental Ballistic Missile (ICBM) program is the most controversial element of Reagan's "strategic modernization program." Since the program entered full scale development during the Carter Administration there has been continuous debate over how many MXs to build, how to base them, and whether they are needed at all. Current plans, recommended by the Presidential Commission on Strategic Forces, call for deployment of 100 MX missiles in existing ICBM silos.(5) This initial deployment is to be followed by additional research on hardening silos to withstand nuclear attack, and the development of a new single warhead ICBM, popularly known as the "Midgetman." The MX will be larger and more accurate than the Minuteman III, the most advanced ICBM currently deployed by the United States. At 193,000 pounds launch weight, the four stage MX is more than two and one-half times as heavy as its three stage predecessor. It will carry 10 independently targetable warheads per missile compared to the three per missile carried by the Minuteman IIIs. Its estimated accuracy of a 400 foot Circular Error Probable (i.e., half of the warheads would be expected to land within a 400 foot radius from their target) would be one and one-half to two and one-half times the estimated accuracy of the Minuteman III.(6)

In the absence of a Freeze, the deployment of more than 100 MX missiles will depend on the fate of the proposed Midgetman program.

Current projections call for a minimum deployment of 1,000 Midgetman small ICBMs beginning in the early 1990s.(7)

The MX missile system has the most complex and extensive prime contracting network of any of the new generation of nuclear delivery vehicles. CEP's *Misguided Expenditure: An Analysis of the Proposed MX Missile System* identifies 37 associate prime contractors and 88 subcontractors for full scale engineering development (FSED) of the MX program.(8) Table II presents the cumulative contract awards to the 14 largest MX contractors for FY 1982, the value of FY 1977- FY 1982 awards, and the work performed and plant location for each contractor.

Of the $7.4 billion in prime contracts awarded for MX work during the FY 1977 through 1982 period, 81.3 percent went to the top ten contractors.(9) Substantial new awards have been made to key contractors since the end of FY 1982: Rockwell International has received over $700 million in additional awards for its work on stage IV of the missile and its guidance and control system; Thiokol was awarded a $310 million follow-on contract for ordnance systems definition and stage IV propulsion; and the Aerojet General subsidiary of General Tire and Rubber was given an additional $246 million award for its work on the missile stage II propulsion system.(10) The most lucrative awards for the system are yet to come: over $30 billion in budget authority for production and deployment of 100 MX missiles and 126 spares is scheduled over the next five years alone. (See Chapter I) Many of these contractors also stand a good chance of winning awards for deployment and production of 1000 'Midgetman' small ICBMs over the next ten to fifteen years if that system goes ahead as currently proposed: the Congressional Budget Office's preliminary estimate of life cycle costs for a 'Midgetman' program is $107 billion.(11)

The Trident II (D-5) Missile

The greatest difference between the proposed Trident II missile and existing Poseidon and Trident I submarine launched ballistic missiles is its increased accuracy. This accuracy will enable the missile to destroy Soviet land-based missiles in their silos as well as other softer military targets. Navy Rear Admiral William A. Williams describes the Trident II's mission in the following terms:

> A sea based missile system that is effective across the entire target spectrum from hard silos, including command and control facilities, to the softer military and war supporting industrial targets...This very characteristic is

essential to our current strategy . . . The Trident II program . . . will provide an increment of invulnerable, hard target kill capability with each submarine that goes to sea.(12)

The Trident II is expected to achieve a Circular Error Probable of 400 feet, comparable to the proposed accuracy of the MX missile system. At 45.8 feet long and 126,000 pounds, the Trident II will be over ten feet longer and almost twice as heavy as the Trident I.(13) For this reason, it can only be accommodated by the Trident submarine with its larger launch tubes. Although the Trident submarine itself is not specifically banned under a Freeze, a Freeze on the Trident II missile would offer an opportunity for Congress to re-consider the Trident submarine program.(14)

According to the *Nuclear Weapons Data Book,* "A minimum of 480 missiles are planned for 20 submarines, with each missile carrying 10 (or more) high yield warheads."(15)

The Trident program is described by one Congressional analyst as "the most expensive US weapons program."(16) According to the Department of Defense's *Selected Acquisition Report,* the total cost of the Trident submarines and Trident I and II missiles will be at least $68.7 billion. Of this amount, $43.7 billion has yet to be authorized by Congress.(17) A nuclear Freeze allows for replacement submarines to be built as long as there is no increase in the number of submarine-based ballistic missile launch tubes or the introduction of any new types of submarine launched ballistic missiles. The size and capabilities of the Trident submarine are more suited to serve as a delivery platform for the counterforce Trident II missile than for maintaining a deterrent balance. Their value or need could conceivably be reconsidered once a Freeze is in force. Nevertheless, in line with CEP's strict interpretation of the Freeze demands, this analysis will focus on the Trident I and II missile programs. The Trident II missile program is projected to cost $37.6 billion, with $35.4 billion yet to be committed.(18)

The Trident I missile entered development in 1974 and was first deployed in 1979. It received its final installment of production funding, $587 million, in the 1983 DoD budget. A total of 570 Trident I missiles will be built.(19) Twelve of the Navy's thirty-one Poseidon submarines have been 'backfit' with Trident I missiles, and the nine or ten Trident submarines that will be deployed between 1983 and 1989 will also be outfitted with these missiles. The combined capabilities of the 12 Poseidons (16 launch tubes each) and the 10 Tridents (24 launch tubes each) account for 408 Trident I missiles. The remainder of the 570 are evidently designed as spares and test missiles. Since the Trident I and Trident II programs have similar contracting networks, and Trident I is already fully funded and deployed in significant numbers, discussion of contractors and system capabilities will be directed at the Trident II.

Lockheed Missiles and Space Company is the principle beneficiary of the Trident missile program to date. From 1973 through the middle of 1982, the firm had received a total of $5.18 billion in contracts on the Trident I and II missile programs.(20) More than half of the company's 8,000 suppliers are involved in the program, and over 50 percent of the dollar value of the work is subcontracted. Most of the 6,500 Lockheed employees in the program work at its Sunnyvale, California plant. A small number of employees, however, are engaged in testing work in Santa Cruz, California and development and integration work at naval bases in Charleston, SC and Bangor, WA.(21) Lockheed received $776.5 million for its work on the Trident I and II missiles in FY 1982, nearly 66.9 percent of the identified prime contracts for this work during that year. Table III presents information on the work performed, contract values, and locations of work for the major contractors of the Trident missile program.

Cruise Missile

Considerably smaller and slower than the other nuclear delivery vehicles, cruise missiles are capable of carrying only one warhead each. Size is a major distinguishing feature of this nuclear weapons system: it ranges from 18 to 21 feet in length and is less than two feet in diameter.(22)

Cruise missiles can be widely dispersed on launch platforms on land, at sea, and in the air. Their small size and physical similarity to non-nuclear missiles create a serious problem of verification in any future nuclear arms agreement. Stationing nuclear armed cruise missiles at sea, on everything from battleships and cruisers to nuclear attack submarines, poses the most difficult problems. It makes almost any ship a potential launch platform for nuclear armed missiles with a range of 1,500 nautical miles.(23)

The terrain contour matching (TERCOM) guidance system, common to all nuclear armed versions of the cruise missile, is designed to make continuous course corrections in the missile's flight path by comparing information on nearby terrain with computer stored maps of the target area. This guidance system is designed to achieve a Circular Error Probable of 100 to 300 feet, making the nuclear armed cruise missiles the most accurate of the new generation of nuclear delivery vehicles (along with the Pershing II).(24)

The idea of the cruise missile is nothing new. In the words of the Navy's Joint Cruise Missile Project Office, "Cruise missile development can be traced back to World War II and its most famous parent, the German-made V-1 buzz bomb."(25) It is essentially a pilotless jet aircraft. The new cruise missiles currently in production and development, however, are smaller, longer in range, and more accurate than those produced in the 1940s and 1950s. Currently, there are 11 different types of cruise missiles under development. All are armed with both nuclear and conventional warheads. Department of Defense plans call for deployment of tens of thousands of cruise missiles over the next ten years at a cost of nearly $30 billion.(26)

The production network for the Air-, Sea-, and Ground-Launched Cruise Missiles is complicated because of overlapping jurisdictions within the armed forces and the introduction of the classified "Stealth" Advanced Cruise Missile (ACM) to replace Boeing's ALCM-B. All cruise missile engine and guidance work is contracted through the Navy's Joint Cruise Missile Project Office, as are the airframes for the ground- and sea-launched versions. The airframe and support equipment for Boeing's ALCM-B is contracted for by the Air Force. The Air Force's Advanced Cruise Missile program contract could go to Boeing, General Dynamics, or Lockheed. The stage of the program and its classified nature, however, make it difficult to determine which firm has the best chance.(27)

Boeing received over $300 million in contract awards for ALCM-B production and the preparation of the B-52s to carry ALCMs during FY 1982. This amount is down from the $689 million received for these two tasks in FY 1981.(28) Engine and guidance work is contracted to the Williams and McDonnell Douglas corporations through the Joint Cruise Missile Project Office.

Contractors for the airframes (General Dynamics), TERCOM guidance system (McDonnell Douglas), inertial reference measuring units and guidance computer (Litton), and the engine (Williams International), received $786 million of the total $921 million identified awards by the Joint Cruise Missile Project Office in FY 1982. This year McDonnell Douglas will have the opportunity to compete with General Dynamics for future airframe contracts. Teledyne CAE of Toledo, Ohio, is a 'strategic second source' for cruise missile engines. It does much of the work on prime contract awards to Williams International for work on cruise missile engines. For example, a $168.8 million award to Williams for 625 F-107 cruise missile engines in early 1983 specified that 33 percent of the work would be done in Toledo by Teledyne.(29) Table IV lists the major contractors for the Ground-, Sea-, and Air-Launched Cruise Missiles (except ALCM airframes), the work they perform, and the value of their FY 1982 contracts.

Pershing II Missile

The Pershing II missile program is the least expensive and the most threatening of all new US weapons programs. The program is currently projected to cost $2.7 billion. The only stated deployment to date is 108 missiles in West Germany.(30) The first was deployed in December of 1983. The Pershing II and the MX deployments have been at the center of the nuclear weapons controversy because of their potential for destroying Soviet military targets.

Martin Marietta, the principal prime contractor for the Pershing II, has received the vast bulk of awards for the program: since 1979, over $1 billion has been awarded to Martin Marietta for work on the Pershing II. It received $351 of the $398 million in identified awards for the system in FY 1982. Table V details the activities of the major prime and subcontractors for the Pershing II missile system.

Nuclear Warheads

Operation of the DoE's nuclear warhead production complex is another major aspect of nuclear weapons production. Operating contracts for the nine largest facilities in the warhead complex run from $94 million per year (for the operation of the Pantex nuclear warhead assembly plant) to over $1 billion (to Union Carbide for running the Y-12 nuclear weapons component plant and three gaseous diffusion plants with civilian and military uses). Profitability, however, is more limited than the size of the contracts indicate. Fees paid over and above operating costs for these facilities range from $8 million to Union Carbide to no fee beyond reimbursement of costs for Dupont's operation of the Savannah River nuclear materials production site.(31) Table VI lists the nine major sites, their operating contractors, and the value of awards for FY 1982 operations. Although the fees above costs are minimal compared with the value of the contracts, these operations involve no investment and no risk to the operating firm, allowing companies to train employees in many aspects of nuclear technology. When Union Carbide announced its decision to let its operating contract for Oak Ridge and the three diffusion plants lapse as of 1986, no fewer than 65 firms applied to replace them.(32) Although warhead work is not as profitable as delivery vehicle production, many corporations clearly see it as being in their best interests to participate.

Exerting Political Influence

The weapons systems described in this chapter yielded $6.6 billion in prime contract awards in FY 1982. In the absence of a Freeze, they will yield tens of billions of dollars in additional contracts through the end of this decade. Over 71 percent of these awards, $4.7 billion, went to the eight largest nuclear weapons contractors: Rockwell International, Boeing, Martin Marietta, Lockheed, General Electric, General Dynamics, McDonnell Douglas, and Northrop. Table VII demonstrates that FY 1982 nuclear weapons contracts accounted for between one and 23 percent of these firms' total sales. Since funding for key systems like the B-1 and MX has accelerated, these firms are probably even more dependent on nuclear contracts now than they were in FY 1982.

As in any business, companies develop a strategy for maintaining and expanding their base. In this case, this multi-billion dollar business has only one customer—the Pentagon. The most viable strategy is exerting political influence over weapons procurement decisions. This is often accomplished by a variety of methods including lobbying, advertising in major media outlets, running grassroots lobbying campaigns, and using Political Action Committee contributions. In fact, military contractors are among the most sophisticated corporations in developing tools for influencing government policy. They have developed an inside track on weapons decisions through the widespread practice of employing former military personnel, supplying members of key defense science and policy advisory committees, and developing new weapons initiatives regularly reimbursed through the Pentagon's Independent Research and Development, Bid and Proposal program. CEP's study of the politics of defense contracting, *The Iron Triangle,* documents these relationships in detail for eight of the largest and most politically active defense contractors. To cite just one example, the eight firms in the study (Boeing, General Dynamics, Grumman, Lockheed, McDonnell Douglas, Northrop, Rockwell and United Technologies) received *one out of every four dollars* awarded by the Pentagon during the decade of the 1970s, and a full 50 percent of their business was from government contracts during that period.(33) Over 1,900 personnel passed between jobs in the Pentagon and armed services and these firms during the period studied, averaging nearly 250 personnel transfers per company. In addition to receiving one out of every three Pentagon Research, Development, Test and Evaluation (R,D,T,&E) dollars during the 1970s, the eight firms had anywhere from 14 to 78 percent of their *independent* R&D programs reimbursed by the Pentagon. The eight firms contributed $2 million to political campaigns from 1976 through 1980, 60 percent of it to federal campaigns.(34) Six of the eight firms covered in the *Iron Triangle* study are among the top eight nuclear weapons contractors described in Table VII.

A Freeze proposal affects a larger array of *new* weapon systems than any arms control proposal brought forward in the past twenty years. The B-1 and Stealth bombers; the MX and Midgetman Intercontinental Ballistic Missiles; the Trident I and II submarine launched ballistic missiles; the Air-, Sea-, and Ground-Launched Cruise Missiles; the Pershing II missile; and the development and production of 17,000 new nuclear warheads would all be postponed under a Freeze. This is very different from arms control proposals such as the 'build down' proposal linked to the Reagan Administration's Strategic Arms Reduction Talks (START). This approach leaves the door open for development and production of new nuclear weapons systems while proposing limits on deployment of older generation systems. The comprehensive and immediate character of a Freeze would close down whole areas of military production for as long as the agreement holds. Corporations heavily involved in the production of nuclear weapons are unlikely to sit still and see a Freeze implemented without fighting back politically.

Rockwell International's successful campaign to revive the B-1 bomber program is the clearest example to date of how a major military contractor can use economic leverage to sustain a program. Under the title of "Operation Common Sense," Rockwell began a campaign in 1973 in support of the B-1 bomber, the Space Shuttle, and the improved Minuteman guidance system. The company spent some $1.35 million on grassroots informational activities supporting the B-1 and the Space Shuttle programs and several California referenda.(35) These activities included several films about the need for the B-1, a B-1 economic impact study, a letter writing campaign among all Rockwell employees which generated over 80,000 messages to Congress in support of the bomber, and ads in *Time, Newsweek, The Wall Street Journal*, and the specialty military press.(36)

This barrage of lobbying activity did not keep President Carter from cancelling the B-1. The company continued its fight for the system by directing political contributions to representatives most likely to revive the program. Most of the firms's $59,625 in campaign contributions from 1977 until President Reagan's announcement of the revival of the program in October 1981 went to B-1 supporters. On the national level, these contributions included $3,500 to Ronald Reagan's presidential campaign, $15,000 to the Republican National Committee, and $25,000 to other Republican committees. More than four-fifths of Rockwell's Congressional campaign contributions went to candidates whose districts included Rockwell plants or to members of key committees with decision making power over military and aviation policies. Forty-two of the fifty-four Rockwell supported members of the House of Representatives voted in favor of the B-1 when it came to a vote in the fall of 1981. Rockwell did even better in key committees: twelve of the fourteen members of the House Armed Services and Appropriations

Committees who received Rockwell campaign contributions voted in favor of the B-1.(37)

Military contractors have already stepped up their political activities considerably in response to growing public criticism of the current military buildup. The Friends Committee on National Legislation determined that twelve of the largest defense contractors spent $1.2 million towards Congressional election campaigns during the 20 month period ending August 31, 1982. This amount represents more than *two and one-half times* the amount these firms previously spent in the comparable period leading up to the 1978 mid-term Congressional elections.(38) The eight largest nuclear weapons contractors spent over $1 million in contributions to Congressional candidates in 1981 and 1982 alone.

Table VIII summarizes the contributions of these eight contractors in the FY 1981–82 period. The eight companies favored Republican candidates by a slight margin of 54 percent to 46 percent of the dollar amounts of their contributions. As did Rockwell during its campaign to revive the B-1 bomber program, each of the firms concentrated heavily on candidates in districts near their major plant locations or on members of key committees with decision making power over weapons programs. In general, the more militarily dependent the firm, the stronger its focus on these two types of contributions: Lockheed, Rockwell, General Dynamics, and McDonnell Douglas each devoted over 70 percent of their contributions to candidates from key geographic locations or members of key congressional committees. Firms with heavier civilian business such as General Electric and Boeing devoted only 50 percent of their contributions to candidates meeting one of these two criteria.

Briefings, advertising, and other techniques are used to complement PAC contributions. Boeing began lobbying for an extension of the ALCM program as soon as the Pentagon announced its decision to cut total purchases of the missile from 3,400 to 1,499. The move toward Stealth cruise missiles could reduce Boeing to the role of a supplier for the program, with the principal prime contract going to General Dynamics or Lockheed. Boeing's strategy for maintaining its cruise missile business includes briefing congressional and Pentagon officials on its views of the benefits of an improved ALCM and entering the competition for the Stealth cruise missile program.(39)

McDonnell Douglas took to the pages of *Time* magazine to advertise the need for cruise missiles. Northrop advertised its role in the MX missile guidance system on the opinion pages of the *New York Times*. United Technologies used a full-page ad in the *Atlantic Monthly* to question the motives of the European peace movement. Advertising the benefits of nuclear weapons extends to employment sections as well. In a special *New York Times* supplement on the "The Employment

Outlook in High Technology" published last year, the bulk of the advertisements from firms seeking employees sang the praises of military systems. Sperry encouraged job seekers to "Join us at Sperry in charting new territories in electronics and computer technology. . .We offer talented professionals a unique opportunity to contribute to exciting programs such as the Trident II FBM Navigation System." The Norden Systems Division of United Technologies asserted that "In Today's Fast Shifting Career World, Your Best Defense is. . .Defense." The ad cited its work in modernizing B-52 radar systems. The February 12, 1984 edition of the *New York Times* ran an advertisement headlined "Engineers—General Electric Wins Record. . .Contract for Trident II." Whether focusing on the 'need' for more nuclear weapons systems or the 'excitement' of designing and building them, these advertising campaigns aim to convince Congress, Pentagon officials, and the general public that these weapons should be a necessary and growing priority of government spending and industrial production.(40)

Some of the most militarily dependent firms have augmented these appeals with pitches to their own employees. Earlier we described Rockwell International's letter writing campaign among its employees which generated 80,000 messages of support for the B-1 bomber program. In September of 1983, Martin Marietta adopted the same tactic in a letter from its President Thomas G. Pownall to all company employees. It appealed to their economic dependency and to a particular vision of national security: "Within the next 60 days the Congress will consider the appropriation of funds for production of the Peacekeeper (MX) missile and other strategic initiatives. These programs are significant to the Corporation. That, of itself, might be reason enough for this communication with our employees, but there are other, higher considerations involved—grave issues of national security which must be decided by the Congress."(41) The letter included preprinted postcards for employees to sign and address to their representatives in Congress. The letter only refers once to the company's substantial stake in nuclear weapons production (over $600 million in Pershing and MX contracts in 1982 alone), and carefully avoids demanding employee participation ("If you agree, and I hope you will. . .please let your Congressman know how you feel."). Nevertheless, appeals of this kind to a firm's employees, particularly if they are accompanied by a 'pep talk' from a supervisor, are often hard to turn down regardless of the employee's position on the issue.

The extent of further lobbying and public relations work by major contractors in the next few years aimed at assuring the continuation of nuclear weapons production remains to be seen.

Footnotes

1. According to a CEP analysis of Office of the Assistant Secretary of Defense, Comptroller, *Procurement Programs (P-1): Department of Defense Budget for Fiscal Year 1984,* and *R,D,T&E Programs (R-l): Department of Defense Budget for Fiscal Year 1984,* $20.7 billion, or 16.8 percent of all DoD procurement and R&D funding, went directly for work on nuclear delivery vehicles, anti-ballistic missile defense, and related support equipment (not counting command, control and communications) in the FY 1984 budget proposal. Department of Defense estimates indicate that 25,000 firms serve as DoD prime contractors, with as many as 100,000 firms involved as prime or subcontractors (conversation of William Hartung with Department of Defense Office of Public Correspondence). If the proportion of funding is a rough guide, over 16,000 firms may be involved as prime or subcontractors for nuclear weapons systems. This estimate, however, does not account for the fact that procurement and research of weapons are not the only things the Pentagon issues prime contracts for—there are substantial contracts let for fuel, foodstuffs, clothing, and other non-weapons items. However, since Rockwell International has asserted that it has 3,000 suppliers for the B-1 program, and Lockheed claims over 4,000 suppliers for the Trident missile program, an estimate of 10,000 firms involved in nuclear weapons production and R&D seems justified (Rockwell's estimate is from an interview with Rockwell International Public Affairs, El Segundo, CA, August 5, 1982; Lockheed's estimate was supplied by G.M. Mulhern, Director of Public Relations, Lockheed Missiles and Space, in a letter to Rochelle Tobias, April 26, 1983). There are 500 suppliers for the B-61 bomb program alone, according to the testimony of Major General William Hoover, in House Armed Services Committee, Procurement and Military Nuclear Systems Subcommittee, *Department of Energy National Security and Military Applications of Nuclear Energy Authorization Act of 1984,* (Washington: US GPO 1983), p. 41. These suppliers are in addition to those who work on DoD nuclear delivery vehicles.

2. US Department of Defense fact sheet, "The Reagan Strategic Program," October 1981. For a discussion of the B-1 cancellation and its reversal by President Reagan, see Gordon Adams, "The B-1: A Bomber for All Seasons?", (New York: Council on Economic Priorities, 1981).

3. Thomas B. Cochran, William M. Arkin, and Milton M. Hoenig, *Nuclear Weapons Data Book: Volume I, US Nuclear Forces and Capabilities* (Cambridge: Ballinger Publishing Co., 1984), p. 162.

4. Interview with Eaton AIL Public Affairs, September 1983, and DoD daily contract award announcements, November 1982 through March 1983.

5. "Report of the President's Commission on Strategic Forces," April 1983.

6. Cochran, Arkin, and Hoenig, *op. cit.*, pp. 118, 121.

7. "President's Commission on Strategic Forces,"*op. cit.*

8. David Gold, et. al., *Misguided Expenditure: An Analysis of the Proposed MX Missile System,* (New York: Council on Economic Priorities, 1981).

9. See Table II for sources of this data.

10. US Air Force, Ballistic Missile Office, Norton Air Force Base, update on MX prime contract awards as of July 31, 1983.

11. Congressional Budget Office, *Modernizing US Strategic Forces: The Administration's Program and Alternatives* (Washington: US GPO 1983), p. 58.

12. *Strategic Force Modernization Programs,* Hearings before the Senate Armed Services Committee, Subcommittee on Strategic and Theater Nuclear Forces, (Washington, DC: US GPO 1981), p. 167.

13. Cochran, Arkin, and Hoenig, *op. cit.,* pp. 142, 145.

14. According to the "Call to Halt the Nuclear Arms Race," the founding document of the Freeze campaign, new submarines may be built during a Freeze as long as the net number of ballistic missile launch tubes at sea are not increased. This would imply that two Trident submarines (24 launch tubes each) could replace three existing Poseidons (16 launch tubes each), as long as no new missiles (such as the Trident II) are deployed with them. Given the cost ($1.5 billion each) of building new Trident submarines, it is conceivable that Congress would decide not to build the full complement under a Freeze, since the missiles they were built to carry (the Trident II) would be forbidden. See footnote 1, introduction to this study, for a full citation on the 'Call to Halt'.

15. Cochran, Arkin, and Hoenig, *op. cit.,* p. 144.

16. Jonathan E. Medalia, "Trident Program: Issue Brief No. IB73001," Library of Congress, Congressional Research Service, December 1, 1973, updated June 17, 1983.

17. Department of Defense, Office of the Assistant Secretary of Defense (Comptroller), "SAR Program Acquisition Cost Summary as of June 30, 1983."

18. *Ibid.*

19. Medalia, *op. cit.,* p. 7.

20. Telephone interview with Lockheed Missiles and Space Co. Public Relations Office, July 14, 1983.

21. *Ibid.*

22. US Navy, Joint Cruise Missile Project Office, "Tomahawk Cruise Missile Facts."

23. See note 26, this chapter.

24. Cochran, Arkin, and Hoenig, *op. cit.,* pp. 177, 180, 187.

25. US Navy, Joint Cruise Missile Project Office, *op. cit.*

26. This estimate was made by Mark Kaplan in "US Cruise Missile Programs," *Arms Control Today* (Washington: The Arms Control Association), May 1983. It includes an estimate of $7 billion for the classified Advanced Cruise Missile program.

27. For a discussion of the competition for the Advanced Cruise Missile contract, see Michael Gordon, "Pentagon's Shift on Cruise Missiles Leaves Big Contractors Scrambling," *National Journal,* March 26, 1983.

28. CEP estimate, based on analysis of Department of Defense, Washington Headquarters Services, DIOR, "Geographic Detail of Department of Defense Prime Contract Awards Above $10,000 Fiscal Year 1981."

29. Department of Defense daily prime contract announcement, December 3, 1982.

30. For background on the Pershing program, see David Gold, "The Pershing II: A Major Threat to Stability," New York, Council on Economic Priorities, November 1983.

31. Information on fees provided by Ken Bertsch, Investor Responsibility Research Center, based on interviews with US Department of Energy information officers.

32. Correspondence between William Hartung and the public affairs department of US Department of Energy, Oak Ridge Operations Office, May 1982.

33. Gordon Adams, *The Iron Triangle: The Politics of Defense Contracting* (New York: Council on Economics Priorities, 1981), p. 35.

34. *Ibid.,* p. 121.

35. *Ibid.,* p. 192.

36. *Ibid.,* p. 193.

37. Gordon Adams, "The B-1: Bomber for All Seasons?," New York, Council on Economic Priorities, February 1982.

38. Friends Committee on National Legislation, "Military Contractors Seek Congressional Access and Influence," Washington, FCNL, November 17, 1982

39. Michael Gordon, *op. cit.,* (see note 27).

40. For a review article on military contractor advertising, see Robert Waters, "Defense Firms Aim at Congress in Ad Blitz," *Hartford Courant,* June 6, 1982. See also "Employment Outlook in High Technology," *New York Times,* section 12, March 27, 1983.

41. Letter from Thomas G. Pownall to Martin Marietta employees, September 12, 1983.

Table I

Major Prime Contractors and Subcontractors for the B-1 Bomber

Company and Location of Work	Goods or Services Being Provided	Amount of Awards FY 1982[a] ($ million)
Rockwell International	(Airframe production and final assembly)	$1,299
El Segundo, CA	Administration, planning, production engineering, and tooling	
Palmdale, CA	Forward intermediate assembly, final assembly	
Columbus, OH	Forward intermediate fuselage, engine nacelles, wing	
Major Rockwell Subcontractors		
AVCO Corporation Aerospace Division Nashville, TN	Manufacture of wings	$200
LTV Corp. Dallas, TX	Aft fuselage, aft intermediate fuselage	$140
Harris Corporation Melbourne, FL	EMUX (electronic multi-plexing) electronic power distribution	$70
Sperry Rand Flight Systems Phoenix, AZ and Albuquerque, NM	Gyroscopic stabilization, back-up flight control system	$30
Boeing Company Seattle and Kent, WA	Offensive avionics system	$278
Major Boeing Subcontractors		
Westinghouse Defensive Division Baltimore, MD	Multi-mode radar/terrain sensor	$145
IBM Corporation Oswego, NY	Central computer, avionics control units, data terminal processor	$50
Sperry Corporation Phoenix, AZ and Albuquerque, NM	Control and display subsystem for offensive avionics	$13

Continued

Company and Location of Work	Goods or Services Being Provided	Amount of Awards FY 1982[a] ($ million)
Sanders, Inc. Nashua, NH	Electronic display units	$12
Singer Company Kearfott Division Little Falls, NJ	Inertial navigation unit	N.A.
General Electric Evendale, OH (Through Engine Division Cincinnati, OH)	F-101-GE-102 engine for B-1	$257
(Detailed data on GE subcontractors not available)		
Eaton Corporation AIL Division Deer Park, NY	Defense avionics system AN/ALQ-161	$198
Major Eaton Subcontractors		
Raytheon Sedco Systems Melville, NY	Electronic countermeasures antenna subsystem	$94
Northrop Defense Systems Division Rolling Meadows, IL	Transmitter, electronic countermeasures systems	$89
General Electric Aerospace Division Utica, NY	Band 8 transmitter	$24

Notes:

a   Amounts of subcontract awards are cumulative awards announced to date, some of which fall outside FY 1982.

Sources: Department of Defense, Washington Headquarters Services, "Alphabetic Detail of DoD Prime Contract Awards Above $10,000, FY 1982"; for subcontract awards, various editions of the *Wall Street Journal* and *Aerospace Daily*, 1982 and 1983, public affairs offices of the major prime contractors and subcontractors.

Table II

Associate Prime Contractors for the MX Missile

Contractor	Goods or Services Being Provided	Awards FY 1977-82[a] ($ million)	Awards FY 1982 ($ million)
Martin Marietta Denver, CO and Vandenberg AFB, CA	Assembly, test and systems support	$1,263.427	$452.295
Northrop		$420.251	$213.984
Electronics Division Hawthorne, CA	Advanced inertial reference sphere (AIRS)	$327.711	$173.210
Precision Products Division Norwood, MA	Third generation gyro for AIRS	$92.540	$40.774
AVCO Systems Division Wilmington, MA	Mark 21 reentry vehicle	$451.841	$99.820
Rockwell International		$1,413.188	$344.659
Autonetics Systems Anaheim, CA	Systems integration: guidance and control system	$856.107	$206.556
Rocketdyne Division Canoga Park, CA		$557.081	$138.103
Thiokol Brigham City, UT	Stage I propulsion system	$616.349	$122.426

Continued

Contractor	Goods or Services Being Provided	Awards FY 1977-82[a] ($ million)	Awards FY 1982 ($ million)
Aerojet General Sacramento, CA	Stage I propulsion system	$545.506	$102.509
Boeing Co. Seattle, WA	Basing	$393.882	$74.552
TRW Co. Redondo Beach, CA	Systems engineering and integration	$282.806	$13.710
GTE Sylvania Systems Group Needham Heights, MA	Command, control and communications systems	$206.325	$60.987
General Electric Reentry Systems Division Philadelphia, PA	Arming and fusing system Mark 12A reentry vehicle	$231.555	$50.428
Hercules Magna, UT	Stage III propulsion system	$362.252	$57.150
Honeywell Clearwater, FL	Specific force integrating receiver accelerometers for AIRS	$797.825	$36.994
Westinghouse Sunnyvale, CA	Launch canister	$55.253	$23.529
Charles Stark Draper Labs Cambridge, MA	Engineering development of guidance and control system	$46.143	$20.013

a For the ten largest contractors, awards are through July 1983.

Source: US Air Force, Ballistic Missile Office, Norton AFB, CA; Department of Defense, Washington Headquarters Services, "Alphabetic Detail of DoD Prime Contract Awards Above $10,000 FY 1982."

Table III

Major Contractors Involved in the Trident Missile
Program

Company and Location	Goods or Services Being Provided	Amount of Contract ($ million)
Lockheed Missiles and Space Sunnyvale and Santa Cruz, CA	Principal prime contractor, final assembly, installation	$776.5
Thiokol, Brigham City, UT and Hercules, Magna, UT (subcontract to Lockheed)	Joint venture to develop first and second stage propulsion systems	NA
Charles Stark Draper Labs Cambridge, MA	Development and engineering design, Trident I Mark 5 stellar/inertial guidance system; development Trident II Mark 6 stellar inertial guidance	$78.7
Singer, Kearfott Division Little Falls, NJ	Production of stellar/ inertial guidance	$38.3
Hughes Aircraft Culver City, El Segundo, and Fullerton, CA	Guidance and inertial measurement unit electronics	$60.1
Raytheon, Sudbury, MA	Guidance and control system components	$26.9
General Electric Ordnance Division, Pittsfield, MA	Guidance system final assembly, Mark 98 fire control system	$43.4
Westinghouse Sunnyvale, CA	Launch canister	$14.8

Sources: DoD, "Alphabetic Detail of DoD Prime Contract Awards Above $10,000", FY 1982; Lockheed Missiles and Space Co.; issues of *Aerospace Daily* and *Aviation Week and Space Technology,* 1982 and 1983.

Table IV

Major Contractors for the Sea-, Ground-, and Air-Launched Cruise Missiles

Company and Location	Goods or Services Being Provided	Amount of Award[a] ($ million)
General Dynamics Convair Division San Diego, CA	Airframe, final assembly for GLCM, SLCM	$341.8
Boeing Company Seattle and Kent, WA	ALCM airframe assembly, GLCM/SLCM production	$108.9
McDonnell Douglas Titusville, FL	Will compete for airframe and assembly contract beginning FY 1984	--
McDonnell Douglas St. Louis, MO	Terrain Contour Matching (TERCOM) guidance system	$217.8
Litton Systems Woodland Hills, CA and Rexdale, Ontario	Inertial navigation elements for ALCM, reference measuring unit/computers for SLCM/GLCM	$61.8
Honeywell Minneapolis, MN	Missile radar altimeter	$2.2
Kollsman Instruments Merrimack, NY	Second source for altimeter, not currently delivering	--
Williams International Walled Lake, MI and Ogden, UT	Engine	$165.0
Teledyne Toledo, OH	Strategic second source, engine subcontractor	N.A.
Atlantic Research Corp. Alexandria, VA	Rocket motor assemblies (boosters)	$7.4
United Technologies Chemical Systems Division Sunnyvale, CA	Rocket motor assemblies (boosters)	$12.1
Westinghouse Sunnyvale, CA	Vertical launch capsule for use in submarines, launch canister	$13.5
Unidynamics St. Louis, MO	Armored Box Launcher (ABL) for use in launching SLCMs for surface ships	$6.8
FMC Corp. Minneapolis, MN	Armored Box Launcher (ABL)	N.A.
Automation Industries Vitro Labs Division Silver Spring, MD	Design of SLCM combat weapon system, shipboard integration system engineering, software	$53.5

Notes:

a All awards for FY 1982 except Atlantic Research Corp. and United Technologies, which are for FY 1983.

Source: Department of the Navy, Joint Cruise Missiles Project Office; US Department of Defense, Washington Headquarters Services, "Alphabetic Detail of DoD Prime Contracts Over $10,000, FY 1982."

Table V

Major Contractors for the Pershing Missile

Company and Location	Goods or Services Being Provided	FY 1982 Award ($ million)
Martin Marietta Orlando, FL	Principal prime contractor; production and assembly	$351.3[a]
Goodyear Aerospace[b] Akron, OH	Guidance system	$7.6
Hercules, Inc. Magna, UT (subcontractor)	Engine	N.A.
Maschinenfabrik Augsburg-Nuernberg, AG Munich, West Germany	Trucks for transport/launch platform	$16.3
Oshkosh Truck Oshkosh, WI	Heavy Expanded Mobility Tactical Trucks (HEMTT) for Pershing IIs to be deployed in the U.S.	$7.7

Note:

a   Over $1 billion awarded to date.
b   Primarily a subcontractor. Figures on subcontracts not available.

Source: Department of Defense, Washington Headquarters Services, "Alphabetic Detail of DoD Prime Contract Awards Above $10,000, FY 1982."

Table VI

Corporate Contractors of the Major Department of
Energy Nuclear Weapons Sites

Site	Contractor	Value of FY 1982 Operating Contract[a] ($ million)
RESEARCH AND DEVELOPMENT SITES		
Lawrence Livermore Laboratories	University of CA	$715.2[b]
Los Alamos Scientific Laboratories	University of CA	$546.3
Sandia Laboratories	Western Electric (subsid. of AT&T)	$795.2
NUCLEAR MATERIALS PRODUCTION		
Gaseous Diffusion Plants Oak Ridge, TN and Paducah, KY	Union Carbide	$1,086.8[c]
Gaseous Diffusion Plant Piketon, OH	Goodyear Atomic	N.A.
Hanford Nuclear Reservation Tri-Cities Area, WA	Rockwell Int'l	$208.3
Savannah River Plant, Aiken, SC	Dupont	$672.5
NUCLEAR WEAPONS PRODUCTION		
Y-12 Plant, Oak Ridge, TN	Union Carbide	$1,086.8[c]
Rocky Flats Plant, Golden, CO	Rockwell Int'l	$270.6
Pinellas Plant Pinellas County, FL	General Electric	$96.0
Mound Laboratory, Miamisburg, OH	Monsanto	$134.5
Kansas City Plant Kansas City, MO	Bendix	$428.9
Pantex Plant, Amarillo, TX	Mason & Hangar – Silas Mason	$94.4

Sources: US Department of Energy, "Awards with a Selected Set of Major Contractors for Awarding Offices 01 Through 05," and "Awards with a Selected Set of Major Contractors for Awarding Offices 06 Through 012," computer printouts as of October 14, 1982. Data originally gathered by Ken Bertsch of the Investor Responsibility Research Center.

Continued

Notes:

a   The operating contract represents the value of awards to the firm for overall management of the DoE facility in question. Some of the sites, such as Hanford, have other contractors involved in specific tasks under prime contracts from DoE, but we have chosen not to list these additional firms in this overview.

b   This contract covers both the management of the Lawrence Livermore nuclear weapons laboratory and the smaller Lawrence Berkeley Laboratory, an energy research laboratory specializing in high energy physics, nuclear physics, and basic energy sciences.

c   This contract covers Union Carbide's management of the diffusion plants at Oak Ridge and Paducah *and* the Y-12 plant and other work at the Oak Ridge, Tennessee, site. As of April 1, 1984, Martin Marietta was the new contractor for these facilities. The limited role of the gaseous diffusion plants in *current* nuclear warhead programs is discussed in Chapter 3 of this study.

Table VII

Dependence of the Eight Largest Nuclear Contractors
on Nuclear Delivery Vehicle Contracts

Contractor	Total Nuclear Delivery Vehicle Awards ($ million)	Nuclear Awards as % DoD Awards	Nuclear Awards as % Total Sales[a]
Rockwell International	$1,644.5	61.1%	21.6%
B-1	1,299.9		
MX	344.6		
Boeing	$875.2	26.6%	9.7%
B-52[b]	488.4		
ALCM	95.9		
GLCM/SLCM	13.0		
B-1B	277.9		
Martin Marietta	$803.6	40.0%	22.8%
MX	452.3		
Pershing	351.3		
Lockheed			
Trident	$776.5	22.2%	13.8%
General Electric	$350.7	9.6%	1.3%
MX	50.4		
GLCM/SLCM	0.262		
B-1B	256.6		
Trident	43.4		
General Dynamics[c]			
GLCM/SLCM	$341.8	5.8%	5.5%
McDonnell Douglas			
GLCM/SLCM	$217.8	3.8%	2.9%
Northrop[d]			
MX	$214.0	13.3%	8.6%

Source: US Department of Defense, Washington Headquarters Services,
Directorate of Information, Operations, and Reports, "Alphabetic Detail
of DoD Prime Contracts over $10,000,   FY 1982."

Continued

a   Company fiscal years do not all coincide with the government fiscal years for which contract information is available, so the military contracts as a percentage of sales may not match figures in company annual reports.

b   This represents all Boeing prime contract awards for work on B-52s in FY 1982. According to company reports cited in Investor Responsibility Research Center, *The Nuclear Weapons Industry* (Washington: IRRC 1984), the firm received $238 million in 1982 (calendar year) for fitting B-52s to carry ALCMs.

c   These figures do not include General Dynamics' awards for work on the Trident submarine.

d   Northrop award figures would be higher if information on awards for its classified "Stealth" bomber work were available.

Table VIII

Political Action Committee Contributions to Congressional Candidates by the Eight Largest Nuclear Weapons Contractors, (FY 1981 and FY 1982)

Company	Total PAC Contributions[a]	% Contributed to Republicans	% Contributed to Democrats	% Contributed to Members of Key Committees or Representatives of Key Geographic Areas[b]
Rockwell International	$ $175,111	67%	33%	72.8%
Boeing	125,400	48%	52%	55.6%
Martin Marietta	131,500	56%	44%	64.3%
Lockheed	184,800	53%	47%	77.5%
General Electric	149,125	52%	48%	51.0%
General Dynamics	172,440	57%	43%	81.5%
McDonnell Douglas	136,675	46%	54%	78.5%
Northrop	101,576	51%	49%	72.8%
TOTAL	$1,176,749	54%	46%	

Source: Federal Election Commission, "Committee Index of Candidates Supported/Opposed, 1981—82''; see other tables in this chapter for sources on contracting date.

Notes:

a Includes only contributions made directly to candidates in Congressional elections. Contributions to Republican and Democratic Committees, and to state and local campaigns, would increase these figures considerably. For example, of $2.1 million in contributions by the PACs of the eight companies in CEP's *Iron Triangle* study made from 1976 through 1980, over $750,000 was contributed in state and local campaigns, and $284,000 went to Republican and Democratic Committees. These figures indicate that the contributions to Congressional candidates listed here may cover only about one-half of each firm's total PAC spending.

b A key geographic area is an area surrounding, or in close proximity to, a major plant location of the firm giving the contribution. Key committees included the Appropriations and Armed Services Committees of both the Senate and House of Representatives; the Subcommittees on Aviation and Science, Technology, and Space of the Senate Committee on Commerce, Science, and Transportation; the Subcommittee on Aviation of the House Committee on Public Works and Transportation; and the Subcommittee on Transportation of the Senate Committee on the Environment and Public Works. This method of analyzing PAC contributions was adapted from Gordon Adams' *The Iron Triangle: The Politics of Defense Contracting* (New York: Council on Economic Priorities, 1981). Full details on the PAC contributions of these companies are available from CEP.

V

The Freeze
And Economic
Conversion

The potential benefits of a Freeze for the national economy are substantial. Freeze savings applied to either civilian government programs or increased consumer spending will result in a net increase in employment. However, even the most effective investment of savings will leave serious problems of adjustment to tens of thousands of workers and scores of communities currently involved in nuclear weapons systems production. The effect of the displacement of as many as 350,000 workers is somewhat softened by their positions as professional and technical workers—a job category with relatively low unemployment rates. Nevertheless, an economic shift of this magnitude will leave many local problems that must be solved. Past experience and current proposals on the economic conversion of military industries and facilities to civilian use provide possible solutions to the problems that will occur as a result of a Freeze.

What is economic conversion? It is a planning process for developing alternative uses of the work force and facilities currently engaged in military production *in advance* of changes in policy that may shut down or slow down work at particular facilities. Different approaches to economic conversion have different emphases. Some concentrate on re-training and financial assistance for affected workers, while others focus on developing a comprehensive process for advance planning with input from all affected parties. More recently, generating alternative sources of investment funds to counter the potential loss of large and regular infusions of Pentagon funding has drawn increased attention from trade unions, community organizations, and state and local elected officials.

Two common themes in all of the approaches to economic conversion reviewed here are job protection and application of actual skills and facilities engaged in military production to alternative civilian activities. These themes distinguish economic conversion from *diver-*

sification, a related strategy for reducing economic dependence on military contracting. Some corporations such as United Technologies have utilized diversification to reduce the share of military production in their overall business base by purchasing civilian firms involved in everything from elevators to computer chips.(1) The state of Connecticut has a law in force designed to attract more civilian businesses to the state and encourage some defense contractors to pursue new civilian product lines.(2) Both of these approaches are diversification rather than conversion efforts because of their failure to focus on advance planning, job protection, and conversion of existing military facilities to civilian uses.

The degree to which government intervention is necessary is an important factor in evaluating approaches to economic conversion. Areas with strong local economies and diversified manufacturing bases need less government assistance than communities where nuclear weapons production is the largest manufacturing activity. However, communities that have devoted their skills and resources to the execution of government military policies deserve some assistance when major policy changes occur. A precedent for this responsibility has already been established for military *corporations*—substantial cancellation fees are written into their contracts with the Department of Defense. Other government programs such as School Aid to Federally Affected Areas (funding local school districts that expanded enrollments to accommodate nearby military bases) have already established that the Federal government should bear some financial responsibility for the economic implications of its military policies.

With this aid comes the necessity to take steps to insure that unnecessary government bureaucracies are not fostered in pursuit of economic conversion. It is important to note that most conversion proposals create new mechanisms for public control over the economic ramifications of decisions by the *existing* bureaucracies in the Department of Defense and the Department of Energy responsible for nuclear weapons system production and deployment.

The cancellation of the B-1 bomber by President Carter in 1977 is a clear example of the need for economic conversion. According to a study conducted by the Department of Defense's Office of Economic Adustment, 6,300 layoffs had already occurred at Rockwell International's Los Angeles area facilities three months after the cancellation. The 1,700 additional layoffs planned along with the multiplier effects of all the layoffs meant an estimated loss of 19,000 jobs in Los Angeles county.(3) The corporation received contract termination payments as part of the cancellation process.

Affected workers and the local community were offered very little in actual resources to cope with the employment cuts and resulting economic disruption. The Freeze proposal will call for cancellation not only of the B-1 but of the Pershing II missile, the Trident I and II missiles, the MX missile, the Air-,Sea-, and Ground-Launched Cruise Missiles, and cutbacks at many of the facilities in the nuclear warhead production complex. As many as 10,000 corporations may be involved as prime or subcontractors. This much broader range of production cancellations poses several times over the problems of the original B-1 cancellation.

The B-1 cancellation is more relevant to evaluating approaches to a Freeze than either the World War II re-conversion or the adjustment to the end of the Vietnam War. The relatively successful re-conversion after World War II was aided by a number of unique circumstances. Pent up demand, resulting from a ten year economic depression followed by wartime full employment with restricted consumer spending, was one such factor. Relatively unchallenged US dominance of post-war international markets was another. In addition, many of the plants undergoing conversion had been involved in civilian production before the war. They were not specialized facilities originally constructed to make weapons.(4) The post-Vietnam reductions in military spending had serious negative consequences in key military production centers such as Seattle. This experience was, however, far more complex than the problems posed by the Freeze. It involved de-mobilization of one and one-half million troops and dramatic drops in Pentagon funding for a wide range of industries that had supplied bombs, ammunition, aircraft and fuel used in the war in Southeast Asia.(5) A Freeze would not affect troop levels and would focus only on a pre-specified set of weapons systems whose production and contracting networks have been described in this report.

The Pentagon's Office of Economic Adjustment (OEA) and the Cabinet level Economic Adjustment Committee are the only existing mechanisms at the Federal level for dealing with military cutbacks. They have had some success in helping communities throughout the country set up industrial parks, educational and recreational facilities, and other civilian projects at former military bases and government arsenals. The OEA's own surveys of the communities it has aided indicate that after a difficult and sometimes lengthly period of adjustment, military sites not only can be reused for civilian purposes, but can provide as many as twice the number of total jobs. An OEA analysis of 94 sites assisted between 1961 and 1981 shows that 123,777 new jobs replaced the 87,703 DoD civilian jobs eliminated through facilities closing.(6)

The readjustment process sponsored by OEA has some applicability to weapons deployment sites which would be affected by a Freeze, but the bulk of the impact of the Freeze will be on military industrial sites. There have been very few success stories in adjustment to major weapons contract cutbacks. Perhaps the most relevant experience is the adjustment to the shifts in weapons production patterns by military prime and subcontractors following the Vietnam War. While many military contractors diversified their operations by expanding civilian product lines (e.g., the aerospace companies) or adding civilian operations through mergers (the route most clearly exemplified by United Technologies), actual examples of conversion of former military industrial facilities or equipment to civilian uses were relatively few and far between. One unique example was Kaman Aerospace, whose owner applied helicopter production technology to the production of the Ovation line of guitars.(7)

Previous efforts make it clear that any attempt to convert nuclear weapons production facilities to civilian uses requires a substantial level of planning and financial support at the Federal, state, and local levels. The most comprehensive approach yet developed nationally is the Weiss conversion bill currently before Congress (H.R. 425). It has historically drawn support from the trade unions with the largest representation in military industries, as demonstrated currently by the support for the bill by the International Association of Machinists.

The Weiss Defense Economic Adjustment Act

Representative Ted Weiss's H.R. 425, the Defense Economic Adjustment Act, is the most comprehensive approach to conversion from military to civilian projects to date. Various versions of this bill have been proposed in Congress every year since 1963. The bill has been refined over the years with input from trade unions most involved in military industrial production. This includes United Automobile Workers' President Walter Reuther's "Swords into Plowshares" proposal in 1969, and substantial support from the International Association of Machinists from the late 1970s on under the leadership of William Winpisinger.(8) The bill has four basic features: 1) a national Defense Economic Adjustment Council; 2) alternative use committees at every defense facility of 100 employees or more; 3) one year pre-notification of a military base closing or major defense contract cutbacks; and 4) financial and re-training assistance for affected workers supported by a trust fund collected from a one and one-quarter percent surcharge on all Pentagon prime contracts. The Defense Economic Adjustment Act represents the most comprehensive planning process for dealing with industrial dislocation resulting from contract cutbacks being seriously considered in Congress.

The Defense Economic Adjustment Council set up under the Weiss bill would be co-chaired by the Secretaries of Labor and Commerce and include other relevant Cabinet members such as the Secretaries of Defense and Energy. Additional representation includes the chairman of the President's Council on Economic Advisors, six representatives of labor organizations, and six representatives of the business community from firms *not* engaged in defense business. The Council's functions will be to encourage Federal agencies to develop concrete plans for national non-defense projects in housing, health care, renewable resources and other areas of national need. It will also coordinate information on priority Federal non-defense projects with the needs and capacities of communities and facilities facing cutbacks in military funds. In addition, the Council will develop a "Conversion Guidelines Handbook" to serve as a resource on civilian job information for displaced military workers. Lastly, the Defense Economic Adjustment Council will be responsible for setting up criteria for determining a community's eligibility for Federal assistance.

Conversion planning at the national level by the Defense Economic Adjustment Council will be complemented at the local level in the Weiss approach by the alternative use committees at each military base and industrial facility of 100 employees or more. These committees, composed of one-half facility management and one-half workers, are charged with responsibility for developing concrete plans for the use of the plant, its equipment, and the skills of the existing work force in civilian production within a maximum period of two years. No plan will be approved unless it "provides for extension of wage, labor, contract provisions, and other benefits to workers at a defense facility until conversion to non-defense-related operations is complete."(9) The penalties laid out in the bill denote the seriousness with which the planning process is taken. "Each contractor which fails to submit an alternative use plan or refuses or fails to carry out the provisions of a plan approved by the Council shall lose eligibility for future defense contracts for a period of three years, lose contract termination payments, and lose eligibility for tax credits."(10)

Assistance for displaced workers provides the necessary bridge between military and civilian employment in converted facilities. It offers a breathing space for workers not employable in the new civilian line of production *or* those displaced from a small facility (100 employees or less) not subject to the planning provisions in the act. While this form of individual assistance is not comparable to a new job at similar wages in civilian production, it provides a wider support system than currently available to any other group of workers in the US facing loss of employment.

Wages of displaced military industry workers will be matched for a period of two years at a rate of 90 percent of the first $20,000 of income and 50 percent of all income above $20,000. Benefits will be paid in the form of economic adjustment benefits *added* to Federal, state, and company unemployment benefits, enabling the worker to reach the specified level of income. Readjustment assistance will also include coverage of any pension and medical benefits the displaced worker received during employment at the affected facility for a period of two years.

Re-training and re-location benefits are another aspect of adjustment assistance proposed in the conversion bill. Workers covered by the adjustment provisions of the bill will be eligible for re-training for civilian jobs of comparable skill and pay levels. Job search and re-location funds to enable them to find and accept such employment will also be available. Managerial and technical employees who spent more than half of the preceding ten years in military industry will be *required* to undergo re-training as a condition of receiving other readjustment benefits. This provision addresses the problem of specialization of skills and managerial techniques within military industry. (11) Re-training programs are designed to undermine management habits developed within the cost-plus, single customer, national security/secrecy environment prevailing in military industries.

The Economic Adjustment Fund is the final major provision of the Defense Economic Adjustment Act. It derives its funds from a 1.25 percent surcharge on all defense prime contracts. Additional funds will come from the deposit in the fund of 10 percent of any projected savings in the military budget as a result of a given cutback or contract cancellation.

How great a potential resource does this involve? If the Weiss bill were passed into law in FY 1985 and was applied to a Freeze on nuclear weapons production to be implemented in 1986, total assets of the fund from surcharges and the 10 percent of projected budget savings would be roughly $5 billion dollars, or over $1,500 per potential displaced worker. This indicates a possible need to appropriate additional funds for the readjustment provisions of the act, at least during the early phases of a Freeze. It also clearly points out the importance of alternative federally supported projects to create the necessary markets for potential production from converted industries.(12)

Most importantly, the Weiss bill will set up a coordinated, federally mandated, and federally financed planning process at every large military facility in the country. Although the greatest potential economic disruption from a Freeze would be relatively concentrated, peripheral effects could touch upon as many as 10,000 of the 100,000 companies involved at some level in military prime or subcontracting. A federally mandated planning process, supported by the executive branch and complemented by local planning committees in all of the communities likely to be affected by contract cutbacks, offers the best chance of avoiding unintended local economic disruption.

The Mavroules Conversion Bill

Representative Nicholas Mavroules (D-MA) has developed a streamlined economic conversion bill currently before Congress as HR 4805. The bill appears to have a better chance of passing in Congress than the more comprehensive Weiss approach. Only two committees have to review it before it can be considered by the full House of Representatives; Armed Services and Education and Labor. Supporters cite this simple review and the fact that it does not call for the establishment of any new government agencies as its key advantages in moving from a bill to a law. The bill is backed by key conversion supporters such as the International Association of Machinists.

The Mavroules approach retains important features of the Weiss bill: one year pre-notification of major contract cutbacks or military base closings, and a two year period of financial and re-training assistance for workers displaced by such cutbacks. Amounts of assistance available to each affected worker are the same as in the Weiss bill.

Key differences between the two bills center on the source of funding for readjustment assistance and the suggested mechanisms for alternative use planning at the national and local levels. Responsibility for administering readjustment and training grants under the Mavroules bill will be vested in the Secretary of Defense, "acting through the Economic Adjustment Committee (established by Executive order 12049, dated March 27, 1978)." Grants supporting planning for alternative production will not be allowed to exceed $250,000 per locality and will only be made "if the Secretary of Defense has determined that such unit is capable of utilizing and is prepared to utilize the amount of the grant for job re-training programs and planning for alternative production."(13) There is no specific readjustment fund as proposed in the Weiss bill—grants to affected workers and communities will be "subject to the availability of appropriations for that purpose" in any given fiscal year.(13)

The Weiss bill calls for mandatory alternative use planning at any major defense facility affected by cutbacks. The Mavroules bill makes planning grants contingent upon whether that unit of local government or the collective bargaining unit of the affected workers is capable of carrying out alternative use planning. In place of the national Defense Economic Adjustment Council proposed in the Weiss bill, the Mavroules approach relies on the existing Economic Adjustment Committee set up during the Carter Administration. This committee, chaired by the Secretary of Defense and including representatives of all major civilian departments of the Federal government, uses the Pentagon's Office of Economic Adjustment as its permanent staff. The OEA's record in helping communities adjust to base closings has been significant. However, in its *twenty years* of operation, the OEA has dealt with situations involving the displacement of only 87,000 civilian employees of the Department of Defense. Dealing with the displacement of as many as 350,000 military industry workers would be an unprecedented challenge to the agency's capabilities, even if it was strengthened by the passage of a conversion act.

It is still an open political question whether Federal conversion legislation will be passed before or in conjunction with the implementation of a nuclear Freeze. While this question remains open, there are some state and local approaches to economic conversion that might be pursued if comprehensive national legislation is not passed in time to cover the economic transition.

State and Local Initiatives

States and localities involved in developing work on alternatives to dependence on military production are those that stand to lose the most if cutbacks were implemented *without* any form of planning or adjustment assistance.

In 1980, the Connecticut state legislature passed "The Defense Readjustment Act of 1980." This act applies a series of existing statewide economic development tools to the problem of defense dependent businesses. Measures required by the act include: 1) giving priority in venture capital assistance provided by the Connecticut Product Development Corporation to defense dependent businesses "whose proposed product or invention is to be used to convert all or a portion of the business to nondefense-related industrial or commercial activity or to create a new nondefense-related or commercial business";(14) 2) making available (through the State Department of Economic Development) tax credits, loans for business expansion, and property tax exemptions for manufacturing facilities in communities where one or more firms have suffered a contract cancellation resulting in unemployment, including financing purchases of machinery and equipment; 3) setting up a statewide Defense Readjustment Task Force consisting of the Commissioners of Economic Development and Labor and the Secretary of the Office of Policy and Management.

The Connecticut act provides for regular monitoring of the degree of defense dependency of the state's economy and brings together private employers with laid off defense contractor employees through job 'task forces.' It also works with local planning agencies in the most defense-dependent areas in the state bringing in new civilian businesses to diversify the local economic·base. Most of the provisions of the Connecticut act provide financial initiatives to businesses (both military and non-military). Their purpose is to encourage production of more civilian products in the state.

The act is the most wide-ranging state government initiative dealing with economic dependence on military contracts yet signed into law. Even so, its provisions are not adequate for dealing with a major shift in the pattern of military contracting in the state. There are no financial benefits to workers, only modest assistance in finding new employers. The wide range of economic benefits offered in the national conversion bills have no counterpart in the Connecticut law. It is difficult for a state receiving almost $6 billion in Pentagon prime contract awards per year to develop an economic strategy and a source of funds that could fully replace any of the larger awards (United Technologies and General Dynamics alone received over $4.5 billion for work in the state in FY 1982). The existing provisions in Connecticut could be helpful in the first phase of a Freeze, since less than 2 percent of the state's prime contracts would be affected.(15) As a Freeze progressed toward actual reductions in nuclear arsenals and the inclusion of dual-capable aircraft and revisions of submarine building plans, as much as 60 percent of the state's contracting could be affected.(16) Perhaps in recognition of the difficulties of the state dealing alone with the larger potential problems of defense dependency, the Department of Economic Development recommended in its most recent review of defense dependency in Connecticut that "State officials. . .support federal legislation designed to ameliorate or lessen the effect of defense spending cutbacks or installation closings on all of those affected."(17)

The Washington State Conversion Project is an alliance of trade union, community, and peace activists. The group began working on economic conversion in the Seattle area six years ago and has developed innovative approaches to financing conversion from military to civilian production and integrating strategies for conversion with broader problems of economic reconstruction at a state level.

When the state's basic industries suffered disproportionately in the current recession, the project applied the concept of conversion to economic reconstruction. Its innovative approaches flow from the problems it encountered.

The approach to state level conversion financing is summed up in the board of director's resolution to focus on "democratizing a substantial portion of Washington State's financial arrangements in order to make money available to peaceful jobs and industries."(18) The most recent proposal is laid out in the pamphlet, *Rebuilding Washington: Converting Corporate Tax Relief into Community Development,* released in March 1983 and adopted as part of the platform of the Washington State Democratic Party. The proposal calls for collecting the $250 million in tax abatements currently offered to corporations by the state government and putting it into job creation programs in public works, job training, and Community Development Finance Corporations. The Finance Corporations will provide venture capital and low interest loans to small businesses and to non-profit Community Development Corporations located in economically depressed areas abandoned by for-profit corporations. The proposal emphasizes creating jobs in the areas of most need (inner cities and underdeveloped rural areas); maintaining a high quality of work life by supporting unionization and withholding state support from firms denying basic employee rights to organization and health and safety protection; and developing local planning institutions to develop projects suited to local needs.

Other financing mechanisms being explored by the Washington State Conversion Project include 1) new state-chartered finance institutions; 2) changes in regulations on investment powers of credit unions; and 3) more democratic control over union pension funds, allowing them to invest in job-creating projects in areas where union members live and work. These financing mechanisms will be applied equally to declining industries (timber production) or to funding conversion from military to civilian production (Boeing's 19,000 defense contract workers or the 5,500 workers engaged in military nuclear operations at Hanford Nuclear Reservation). This ambitious approach to economic reconstruction, state level financing, and local alternative planning appears more suited to the scope of the conversion problem. It includes striving for substantial funding alternatives to replace billions of dollars of military contracts and, in terms of its broader political appeal, economic reconstruction of the state as a whole. These types of regional initiatives will be important for any workable program of conversion on a national scale.

California's "Silicon Valley," another highly defense dependent area, has taken the lead in developing approaches to conversion. The Mid-Peninsula Conversion Project, active in the area for eight years, has developed an approach to utilizing the skills and facilities from the area's military electronics sector to develop a solar energy industry. The result, *Creating Solar Jobs,* remains the most comprehensive local example in the US of "alternative use planning."(19) It enlists all groups affected by military production in developing plans for civilian uses of the available skills, plant, equipment, and community resources. The project involved military industry workers, local trade unions (including the Machinists Union local at Lockheed that builds the Trident II missile), community organizations, and local officials in the development of the alternative plan. The project continues to develop alternative use planning at the county and city level with community organizations, technical professionals, and workers at military plants. Most recently, the United Auto Workers local at the Long Beach, California plant of McDonnell Douglas Corporation is working with the project on a range of alternative products (ranging from commuter aircraft, to light rail vehicles, to energy cogeneration equipment) that could be produced there. Other applications of alternative use planning by the product included a Jobs in Energy Project, which brought together low-income residents of East San Jose, solar designers, and members of the local building trades council to apply solar and conservation techniques to resident's homes.

A relatively new approach to local conversion problems is the local conversion fund. Bishop Leroy Mathiessen of Amarillo, Texas began a fund for workers at the Pantex nuclear weapons assembly plant who wish to leave their jobs as a matter of conscience but see little alternative in the local economy. The Knolls Action Group in the Albany area of New York State has a similar fund for employees at the General Electric operated Knolls Atomic Laboratories, who develop naval reactors and train operators for the reactors in the new Trident submarines. At the national level, the Reformed Church in America is discussing a proposal to establish a Peacemaking Pastoral Support Fund to provide professional counsel and financial aid to persons who decide for reasons of conscience to cease employment in occupations related to the production and deployment of nuclear weapons.

Most conversion supporters believe creating alternative sources of employment is more important than getting individuals involved in nuclear weapons production to leave their jobs. The Atomic Reclamation and Conversion Project, started by members of Oil Chemical and Atomic Workers union local 3-689, is actively promoting this approach. The project is aimed at converting the DoE's Piketon, Ohio gaseous diffusion plant site into a new civilian industrial activity within the next ten years. The plant enriches uranium for nuclear power reactors and serves as a standby source of enriched uranium for use in nuclear weapons—the development of new, less energy intensive techniques of uranium enrichment threatens both of these functions by the early 1990s.

Another approach to creating alternative employment is to provide new investment outlets for institutions that traditionally invest funds in military corporations. The New York based Coalition for Responsible Investment, long involved in using shareholdings of religious organizations to raise issues of peace and economic conversion with military corporations, has an alternative investment fund in the New York, New Jersey, and Connecticut area. This fund offers alternative uses for church funds currently invested in military corporations. The projects supported by the fund will "meet the unmet basic human needs of food, shelter, education, health, and jobs."(20)

Conversion, Recession, and 'Reindustrialization'

Critics of economic conversion tend to focus on either its political feasibility (can national legislation be passed?) or its alleged cost and complexity (wouldn't it require a costly and cumbersome bureaucracy?). The first criticism must be viewed in the light of the popularity of the Freeze itself: in public opinion polls, in the Congress, and in public referenda, it has received more consistent and widespread support than any disarmament initiative of the past twenty years. Even after the recent Soviet attack on Korean Airlines flight 007, hailed in the media as a striking blow to the Freeze and other arms control initiatives, pollster Louis Harris found 77 percent of the American public supporting a bilateral Freeze.(21) If economic conversion legislation were reintroduced in Congress with the full backing of the Freeze campaign, major unions like the Machinists, AFSCME, and the National Education Association, and religious denominations that have taken a stand against nuclear weapons production, its chances of success would be considerably better than in past years.

Regarding the question of complexity and bureaucracy—there is no more difficult bureaucracy to understand and control than the one currently existing within the Pentagon and the Department of Energy for the research, testing, production, and deployment of nuclear weapons. Conversion legislation offers a measure of public input and control over this existing bureaucracy. Most importantly, it would free defense dependent communities from the current option of lobbying for more weapons contracts or facing heavy losses of income and employment.

Another implicit criticism of economic conversion planning is that it offers assistance and security to one group of relatively well paid workers that is not available to workers in declining civilian industries, the service sector, or to poor and unemployed people. A broader approach to conversion as a part of a process of democratic reconstruction of the whole economy, proposed nationally by the International Association of Machinists and regionally by organizations like the Washington State Conversion Project, addresses this criticism. The most important potential economic benefit of a nuclear Freeze is the opportunity to use Federal funds, research and production facilities, and the skills currently engaged in nuclear weapons testing and production to solve some of the nation's pressing economic problems. The "Defense Economic Adjustment Act" offers: 1) a mechanism for planning that covers every major military facility in the country; 2) a coordinating body to steer priority Federal projects to areas adjusting to military cutbacks; and 3) a series of financial and training benefits for affected workers. It *does not* guarantee comparable employment at comparable wages. It *does offer* a better chance of achieving this goal. Missing from even the most comprehensive conversion legislation is a regular source of investment and markets comparable to the $100 billion plus spent every year by the Pentagon on weapons and supplies. The Weiss bill conversion fund accumulates at a rate of 1 and ¼ percent of total Pentagon contracts per year. This may not even cover all of the potential worker benefits demanded by Freeze related contract cutbacks, much less provide any form of steady investment or procurement funds from the Federal government to affected communities. Investment funds and markets necessary to make conversion work most effectively must come from within a larger framework. One such approach is contained in the International Association of Machinists' "Rebuilding America Act."

The Rebuilding America Act

William Winpisinger, President of the International Association of Machinists, defined the difference between existing conversion and reindustrialization plans and his union's proposed "Rebuilding America Act" in the following terms:

> "When the economy crashes upon millions of working men and women, as any economy tailored to the greed of corporate power must, we intend to be ready. This means we are refining, improving and expanding our legislative model for economic conversion...we intend to be ready with a comprehensive program of economic reconstruction.
> ...In addition to breaking the bonds of economic necessity that now keep so much of the work force captive to war production, the concept of economic reconstruction extends to the far greater and more fruitful task of rebuilding America."(22)

The main feature which distinguishes the Machinists' Union "Rebuilding America" plan from other 'reindustrialization' plans is corporate accountability to the workers and communities that provide these corporations' profits. The Machinists plan ties government supported loans and specific tax breaks to corporate recognition of trade union organizing rights, health and safety regulations, minimum wage laws, and a *commitment* to remain in the community unless it is proven unprofitable to do so. The act goes so far as to set up a procedure for a company to show just cause for not being able to operate in a given area before it can move. It can be enjoined from moving if it fails to show sufficient cause. This aspect of the act applies the commitment to community economic security entailed in the Machinists' support for conversion planning to the whole range of problems of economic dislocation.

More importantly, the Machinists' plan proposes two funding mechanisms capable of supporting alternative industrial production—the existing Federal Financing Bank and a new Pension Fund Development Bank. It also offers several possible structures for carrying out this production in addition to the existing military corporations. It is in this area of creating structures for funding alternative production that the "Rebuilding America Act" has the most to offer. By proposing an institutional commitment to funding infrastructure, energy, housing, and other key civilian investments, the Machinists plan offers the possibility of accomplishing the transition from permanently high military spending with maximum economic benefits for affected workers and communities, as well as the entire national economy.

Conclusion

It is clear that almost any other form of spending in equivalent amounts is better for overall employment and availability of needed goods and services than continued nuclear weapons production. Of the various possible alternatives, not all necessarily require the same skills or must be carried out in the same locations. The comprehensive form of conversion planning and economic adjustment assistance proposed in the Defense Economic Adjustment Act offers the best alternative for easing the transition of defense dependent communities and workers to civilian production. This planning process will be particularly helpful in handling a change in military policy with the decisive industrial impact of a nuclear Freeze.

However, advance planning, re-training, and financial assistance do not guarantee new jobs at comparable wages for all defense industry workers affected by the Freeze. Proposals such as the Machinist's "Rebuilding America Act," focusing on publicly accountable mechanisms for funding new civilian investments on a consistent basis, complement conversion planning proposals by supplying the most important missing link: a potentially guaranteed source of civilian investment and purchasing power to replace the tens of billions of dollars per year currently devoted to nuclear weapons production.

Going ahead as planned with the construction of a new generation of nuclear weapons also has its costs. The current method of funding the nuclear buildup destroys jobs and services at a steady pace. These costs far outweigh the economic benefits of building warheads and missiles. A Freeze offers many opportunities for service restoration, public employment and investment programs, or reduction of burgeoning Federal government deficits. The question is not "Can a Freeze benefit the economy?," but "How can the economic benefits of a Freeze be maximized?" A responsible approach to this question must take into account the needs of workers and communities currently depending on nuclear weapons systems production for their livelihood.

Footnotes

1. For statistics on the changing proportion of civilian products within United Technologies' business base, and an overview of its diversification efforts, see Gordon Adams, *The Iron Triangle: The Politics of Defense Contracting* (New York: Council on Economic Priorities, 1981), pp. 422, 425–26.

2. Connecticut State Legislature, *The Defense Readjustment Act of 1980.*

3. Department of Defense, Office of Economic Adjustment, *Economic Impact on Los Angeles County of the Curtailment of the B-1 Bomber Program,* 1977.

4. For discussions of the effects of the World War II buildup and its aftermath, see Seymour Melman, *The Permanent War Economy: American Capitalism in Decline* (New York: Simon and Schuster, 1974); Philip Webre, *Jobs to People: Planning for Conversion to New Industries* (Washington, D.C.: National Center for Economic Alternatives, unpublished); Betty Goetz Lall, *Prosperity Without Guns* (New York: Institute for World Order, 1977): and Paul Baran and Paul Sweezy, *Monopoly Capital: An Essay on the American Economic and Social Order* (New York: Monthly Review Press, 1977).

5. For background on the Vietnam de-mobilization and its economic implications, see Seymour Melman, editor, *The War Economy of the United States* (New York: St. Martin's Press, 1971); *Postwar Economic Conversion: Hearings Before the Committee on Labor and Public Welfare, United States Senate,* 2 volumes (Washington: US GPO, 1970); *National Economic Conversion Commission: Responses to Subcommittee Questionnaire,* Committee on Government Operations, US Senate, (Washington: US GPO, 1970); and Paul Joseph, *Cracks in the Empire: State Politics and the Vietnam War,* (Boston: South End Press, 1981).

6. Department of Defense, Office of Economic Adjustment, "Summary of Completed Military Base Economic Adjustment Projects: 1961-1981, 20 Years of Civilian Reuse," Washington, DC, US Department of Defense, November 1981.

7. "Kaman: How to Bring Aerospace Knowhow to the Guitar Industry," *Business Week,* June 26, 1978; William H. Gregory, "Kaman Plucking Profits from Guitars," *Aviation Week and Space Technology,* August 5, 1974.

8. On the UAW role, see Walter Reuther, *Swords into Plowshares: A Proposal to Promote Orderly Conversion from Defense to Civilian Production,* (Detroit: United Automobile Workers, 1969). For a recent Machinists' Union statement on the subject, see William Winpisinger, "Organized Labor and Economic Conversion," in Lloyd Dumas, ed., *The Political Economy of Arms Reduction* (Washington: American Association for the Advancement of Science, 1982).

9. "The Defense Economic Adjustment Act," 97th Congress, 2nd Session, H.R. 425, 1983.

10. *Ibid.*

11. For discussion of this point see Melman, *The Permanent War Economy,* op. cit., and US Arms Control and Disarmament Agency, "The Transferability and Re-training of Defense Engineers," November 1967.

12. The assets of the fund are calculated on the following assumptions: total DoD contract awards for FY 1985 will be $200 billion, yieldig a 1.25% surcharge of $2.5 billion; and Freeze savings for FY 1985 will be roughly $25 billion including savings in delivery vehicles and warheads, yielding a 10% increment of $2.5 billion for the readjustment fund. This would yield total assets of $5 billion as of the beginning of FY 1986, which would in theory be added to by surcharges on contracts awarded during 1986. The bill states that "The Secretary of the Treasury shall determine the projected savings in defense spending as a result of cancellation or cutback of a program or contract and shall deposit 10 per centum of the projected savings in the fund." We used the conservative assumption that the 10% would be applied to the amount of budget savings during the year the programs are cancelled. If the savings

were projected over more than one year, the contribution to the fund would rise substantially; for example, a three year estimate of Freeze savings (1985–87) of $67 billion would yield a $6.7 billion contribution to the fund.

13. "The Economic Conversion Act," HR 4805, US House of Representatives, 1984.

14. "Connecticut Re-adjustment Act of 1980," op. cit.

15. Marta Daniels, Kevin Cassidy, and Kevin Bean, "The Effects of a Nuclear Weapons Freeze on Connecticut's Economy", Connecticut Campaign for a US-Soviet Nuclear Weapons Freeze, 1983.

16. *Ibid.*

17. Connecticut Department of Economic Development, report on the Defense Re-adjustment Act (untitled), December 1982, p. 4.

18. Washington State Conversion Project, *Conversion Perspectives,* October/November 1982, "Director's Corner".

19. Mid-Peninsula Conversion Project, *Creating Solar Jobs: Options for Military Workers and Communities* (Mountain View, CA: MPCP 1978).

20. Coalition for Responsible Investment, "The Alternative Investment Fund of the Tri-State Coalition for Responsible Investment," statement of principles, 1983.

21. Louis Harris poll, cited in the *St. Louis Globe-Democrat,* September 29, 1983.

22. William Winpisinger, address before the American Association for the Advancement of Science, reprinted in full in Lloyd J. Dumas, ed., *The Political Economy of Arms Reduction* (Washington: AAAS 1983). For a full statement of the Machinists' position, see *Rebuilding America,* (Washington: International Association of Machinists, 1983).

Summary of Findings

The fate of the nuclear Freeze proposal should rise or fall on its merits as a means of reducing the risks of nuclear war. Unfortunately, defense and security are not always the decisive factors in determining which weapons get built. The economic benefits of programs such as the B-1 bomber and the C5-A cargo plane have contributed significantly to their success.

A Freeze would cancel more new weapons programs than any other nuclear arms control initiative of the past twenty years. To explore the economic consequences, CEP analyzed the budget savings from a nuclear Freeze, its costs in jobs and income for the workers and communities currently dependent upon nuclear weapons system production, and the net effects of applying the savings elsewhere. Understanding the economic effects of a halt in nuclear weapons production in advance can enable the US to minimize the economic disruption and maximize the economic benefits of its implementation.

Chapter I: Budget Savings From a Nuclear Freeze

The $98 billion in budget savings that could be realized in the next five years is the most visible economic benefit of a Freeze. If a Freeze holds, the initial savings would grow to over $400 billion by the end of this century. The short-term calculation is a minimum estimate, based on a strict and narrow interpretation of the systems immediately affected by a Freeze.

Major short-term savings would result from the cancellation of development and production funding for the MX and Trident ballistic missiles, the Pershing II missile, the Air-, Sea-, and Ground-Launched Cruise Missiles, and the B-1B bomber. Cancellation of the B-1, MX, and Trident II programs alone would provide just under *two-thirds* of the total savings. Termination of nuclear warhead production and development currently carried out by the Department of Energy would yield $21 billion of the $98 billion that could be saved in the next five years.

Further budget savings could be realized in both the short- and the long-term beyond those documented here. Spending on classified programs (the Stealth bomber and Advanced Cruise Missile) and new proposals that do not yet have detailed funding projections (the Midgetman small ICBM) would also be terminated under a Freeze. This adds a substantial but unknown amount to the five year savings projections. If a Freeze leads to actual reductions in nuclear arsenals, there could be tens of billions of dollars saved on maintenance and deployment of nuclear systems. Finally, a mutual Freeze would call into question the need for many related programs: strategic air and ballistic missile defense; command, control and communications for a prolonged nuclear conflict; and delivery platforms (such as the Trident submarine) which are primarily designed to carry new, more accurate nuclear armed missiles.

Chapter II: Effects of a Nuclear Freeze on Employment

Displacement of workers in military industry is the most immediate economic problem posed by a nuclear Freeze. CEP estimates based on Bureau of Labor Statistics employment requirements tables indicate that a Freeze could displace between 250,000 and 350,000 workers. These projections are only a part of the picture. Freeze budget savings applied elsewhere—to reducing Federal deficits, to funding other Federal programs, or to cutting taxes—would produce a net *increase* in overall employment, according to a series of studies by government and private economists.

A Freeze need not increase unemployment. An econometric analysis by the Congressional Budget Office indicates that $10 billion in government expenditures on weapons procurement in Fiscal Year 1983 would have produced 40,000 *fewer* jobs than if the same $10 billion were spent on civilian government programs *or* general military spending (including military personnel). Applying these findings to a Freeze, CEP found that a shift of its budget savings to civilian programs in FY 1984 could increase overall employment by 50,000 jobs. Both the Employment Research Associates (ERA) and Chase Econometrics have done studies demonstrating that cutting nuclear weapons related spending and applying the savings to a tax cut would increase overall employment levels. Using input-output analysis, ERA found that as of 1981, $1 billion in spending on nuclear weapons systems created 24,000 jobs. The same billion dollars spent by consumers on goods and services would create an average of 38,000 jobs. Adjusting these results to the effect of a Freeze with a compensating tax cut in FY 1984, CEP estimates that overall employment could increase by as much as 150,000. The magnitude of the net gain in employment will depend on how consumers and businesses respond to initial changes in the pattern of demand for goods and services. These responses will vary depending upon the general health of the economy. Nevertheless, the consensus of the major studies in the field is that employment should increase if weapons cutbacks required by a Freeze are compensated for by equivalent levels of government or private demand.

What if Freeze cutbacks are not compensated for by other forms of spending? Cutting Federal deficits with savings from a Freeze would address the fears of many government and business economists that consistently high government borrowing could short circuit economic recovery. However, there is no strong evidence that such a move would offer immediate benefits in offsetting employment displacement. Under this worst case, less than 0.4 percent of the nation's workforce would be affected. Whether there is a net increase or net decrease in employment under a Freeze, it is important to know which industries and services would bear the brunt of job displacement; what *types* of jobs will be affected; and the regional distribution of nuclear weapons related employment.

Contrary to popular assumption, jobs in basic industries like steel (already hard hit in recent years) would *not* be heavily impacted by Freeze related cutbacks. Outside the traditional military supplying sectors of aircraft, guided missile production, radio and TV communications, and electronics, the bulk of indirect employment stimulated by nuclear delivery vehicle production is in business services, eating and drinking places, hotels and lodging places, and retail trade. This reflects the tremendous expenditures by military contractors on lobbying, preparing bids and proposals, and other public relations efforts.

Even within the direct production of missiles, bombers, and warheads, the job categories most heavily affected would be professional and technical positions. Industries most directly affected by a Freeze employ three to six times as many professional and technical personnel as the average manufacturing industry. These categories have unemployment rates well under one-half of the national average. Conversely, nuclear weapons industries employ ½ to ¼ as many operatives and laborers as the average industry. These positions have been hit hardest by unemployment, with a rate nearly twice the national average.

Production of nuclear delivery vehicles and warheads is highly concentrated regionally. California alone receives over half of the prime contract awards for the major missile and bomber programs covered by the Freeze. In Fiscal Year 1982, the top five states received over 76 percent of Freeze-related prime contracts, and the top ten states received over 94 percent of these awards (see Table I). The vast majority of states—39 in all—received between 0 and $100 million in prime contracts that would be affected by a Freeze. Delivery vehicle subcontractors, divisions or subsidiaries of major prime contractors, or Department of Energy-owned warhead production sites in some of these states would face adjustments. Estimating the full impact in the 39 remaining states requires systematic government reporting of subcontract awards. CEP has been able to identify less than 2 percent of the 9,000 to 10,000 subcontractors involved in nuclear weapons system production. Full government reporting of first and second tier Department of Defense and Department of Energy subcontracts is necessary to fully plan the economic transition to a Freeze. In the absence of this information, CEP's findings on the narrow distribution of prime contracts offer a clear indication that most states would not suffer major economic displacement from a halt in nuclear weapons production.

Chapter III: The Opportunity Costs of the Nuclear Weapons Buildup

The net economic effect of a Freeze will depend heavily on how budgetary resources freed up by a halt in nuclear weapons production are applied. There are a variety of competing claims for Federal revenues. CEP has examined the three alternatives that have strong support from key constituencies—community organizations, state and local government officials, trade unions, and the business community:
1) Restoration of basic human services programs;
2) Public investments in housing, mass transit, infrastructure, and employment and training programs;
3) Cutting Federal government deficits.

Restoring Basic Human Services: Freeze savings could restore all of the budget cuts since 1981 in Aid to Families with Dependent Children, Food Stamps, child nutrition, *all* Federal education programs, the Social and Community Services Block Grants, and the Occupational Safety and Health Administration. These programs, serving tens of millions of Americans, could be restored to 1981 levels and protected against inflation for the next five years using budget outlay savings from a nuclear Freeze. This would still leave $11 billion free for re-adjustment and re-training assistance and planning grants for workers and communities affected by a halt in nuclear weapons production.

Public Investments: Freeze budget savings could make a substantial contribution to public investment and public employment programs. The FY 1984 Freeze savings alone could support the construction of

170,000 new housing units, and a jobs program for 430,000 unemployed teenagers. By creating jobs for teenagers and construction workers, these programs would create jobs for those who need them the most.

Cutting the Deficit: If Freeze savings were used to cut government spending, Federal government deficits could be reduced by $13 to $21 billion per year for each of the next five years, for an annual percentage reduction of 7 to 12 percent each year. This compares favorably with proposals for cutting deficits through spending reductions proposed by organizations such as the Bi-Partisan Appeal on the Budget Crisis (which includes six former US Secretaries of Commerce). Deficit reductions from a Freeze would be largest in Fiscal Year 1986, the period during which many economists fear that government borrowing may short circuit economic recovery. Although Freeze savings alone cannot eliminate deficits, they could be a key factor in *equitably* cutting deficits through reductions in military as well as civilian programs.

Applying Technical Talent to Civilian Problems: A Freeze opens up possibilities for alternative applications of the skills and specialized facilities currently devoted to nuclear weapons system production. *At least* 5 to 8 percent of US scientists and engineers are currently engaged in work on nuclear warheads, nuclear delivery vehicles, and related command and control equipment. This significant pool of technical talent could be put to work solving problems in energy, pollution control, safe disposal of chemical and nuclear wastes, and other pressing areas of national need.

The US Department of Energy most clearly exemplifies the current shift of government resources toward military programs. As a result of its responsibility for the design, production, and testing of all US nuclear warheads, coupled with the Reagan Administration's preference for free market solutions to energy programs, military programs have grown from 30 to 53 percent of the DoE's budget from 1981 to 1984. A Freeze on warhead production would allow a thorough re-evaluation of the Department's commitment to alternative and renewable energy programs that have suffered the deepest cuts of any DoE programs over the past three years.

Chapter IV: The Corporate Role in Nuclear Weapons Production

Although over 10,000 firms are involved in some aspect of nuclear weapons production, the awards are highly concentrated. Of the $6.6

billion in Department of Defense prime contract awards for the major nuclear delivery vehicles in FY 1982, *the top eight contractors received 71 percent of the total* (see Table II). Even allowing for subcontracting, which often redistributes as much as 50 percent of a major award to supplier firms, these eight firms are clearly the major financial beneficiaries of nuclear weapons spending.

Nuclear weapons system contracts are a substantial and growing part of the total sales of the largest contractors: for Rockwell (B-1, MX), Boeing (B-1, Cruise missiles), Martin Marietta (MX, Pershing II), and Lockheed (Trident missile) between one-tenth and one-fifth of their total FY 1982 sales were accounted for by contracts for the major nuclear delivery vehicles. A Freeze now would probably affect an even larger share of the sales of these firms, since in FY 1982 (the most recent year for which systematic breakdowns are possible) several of the larger nuclear delivery vehicle programs were still in the research and development stage. Contracts are smaller at this stage than after full scale production begins.

These contractors have developed a number of mechanisms for exerting political influence in favor of their weapons programs. The most visible campaign was carried out by Rockwell International from the mid-1970s on in support of its B-1 bomber. The company waged a sophisticated public relations effort using economic impact studies, media advertising, an employee letter writing campaign, and regular campaign contributions to members of key Congressional committees. This campaign was instrumental in getting the B-1 program restored after its 1977 cancellation by the Carter Administration. Evidence of similar efforts by other major contractors is less conclusive, but at least one firm, Martin Marietta, has used the employee letter writing campaign in support of its MX missile program.

The most systematically documented technique used by all major contractors is the Political Action Committee (PAC) contribution. In 1981 and 1982, the eight largest nuclear weapons system contractors contributed a total of over $1.1 million to candidates for the Senate and House of Representatives. The bulk of these contributions, between 55 and 81 percent for each firm, went to members of key committees with decision making power over weapons programs or to candidates from locations near contractor plants with signficant amounts of military work. Republicans received 17 percent more funding from these firms than Democrats.

Chapter V: The Freeze and Economic Conversion

Even the most effective investment of savings from a nuclear Freeze will leave serious problems of adjustment for tens of thousands of workers and scores of communities currently involved in nuclear weapons production. The disruptive effects of a Freeze will be mitigated by three factors mentioned in this study:

1) If Freeze savings are returned to consumers in the form of a tax cut or spent on civilian government programs, overall employment will rise.

2) Job displacement will be heavily skewed towards scientific and technical job categories with unemployment rates less than one-half of the national average.

3) The vast majority of states will suffer little or no negative economic impacts from the implementation of a Freeze—the bottom forty nuclear weapons contracting states received only 6 percent of these awards in FY 1982.

Although these factors make the economic transition from nuclear weapons system production easier, many potential problems remain. The extent of long-term displacement will depend upon whether Freeze cutbacks are compensated for by equivalent civilian spending. Even under the best possible macroeconomic adjustment, there is a need for special re-adjustment measures to aid communities which are heavily dependent upon nuclear systems production for jobs and income.

To address this transition problem, CEP reviewed several approaches to economic conversion, the process of planning for the civilian use of skills and facilities no longer needed for military purposes. The widespread and immediate character of a Freeze, affecting as many as 350,000 workers involved in production of nuclear warheads, missiles and bombers, mandates a nationally coordinated approach to minimize local economic disruption after a Freeze. Federal assistance to help soften the adverse affects of changes in military policy has numerous precedents. They include the work of the Pentagon's Office of Economic Adjustment in helping communities adjust to military base closings and the regular practice of providing substantial contract termination payments to corporations upon cancellation of DoD weapons programs.

Critics of conversion planning argue that the normal operation of the labor market is the best mechanism for handling displacement due to changes in military policy. Corporate and Pentagon officials also argue that comprehensive conversion planning approaches would foster an unnecessary bureaucracy.

These arguments ignore the fact that defense contracting is not a 'free market' activity. Conversion planning offers a measure of public control over the economic effects of decisions made by the *existing* bureaucracies in the Pentagon and Department of Energy responsible for weapons procurement decisions. While it is important to ensure that conversion planning mechanisms operate as smoothly and efficiently as possible, the need for some form of Federal planning process to deal with economic adjustments to major policy changes like the Freeze is clear.

There are currently two economic conversion bills before the Congress. The most comprehensive approach, sponsored by Rep. Ted Weiss (D-NY) is the Defense Economic Adjustment Act, HR 425. The Weiss bill has four major provisions:

1) Establishment of a national Defense Economic Adjustment Council, co-chaired by the Secretaries of Commerce and Labor, to develop concrete plans for non-military projects in key areas of national need that could be steered to areas affected by defense contract cutbacks or base closings;

2) Mandatory alternative use committees composed of workers and management for any military base or defense plant with 100 employees or more;

3) One year pre-notification of base closings or major contract cutbacks:

4) Supplemental unemployment benefits, re-training assistance, and planning grants for workers and communities affected by defense program cutbacks, to be drawn from a "Workers Readjustment Reserve Trust Fund" built up from a 1.25 percent surcharge on all DoD prime contract awards.

The economic conversion bill proposed by Rep. Nicholas Mavroules (D-MA) is HR 4805. It provides for pre-notification of contract cutbacks and worker re-training and re-adjustment assistance comparable to those of the Weiss bill. However, it makes alternative use planning dependent upon the initiative of local units of government and has no 'reserve fund' of the type proposed in HR 425. The Mavroules approach puts administration of conversion programs in the hands of the President's Economic Adjustment Committee, an existing agency chaired by the Secretary of Defense and supported by the DoD's Office of Economic Adjustment. The less comprehensive Mavroules bill is thought to have a better chance of gaining Congressional approval.

A number of state and local initiatives already underway could offer some means for easing the economic transition required by a Freeze. Connecticut has passed a "Defense Re-Adjustment Act" that focuses on diversifying the state's economic base by offering tax and credit incentives to firms to move into civilian product lines and/or locate in communities where defense contract cutbacks have resulted in unemployment. The Washington State Conversion Project has won the endorsement of the state's Democratic party for a proposal that would set up a series of new tax and credit sources to promote civilian economic development in areas affected by defense contract cutbacks or declining civilian industries. Several *local* alternative use planning initiatives have been started by workers at defense facilities. In conjunction with the Mid-Peninsula Conversion Project, members of the United Auto Workers (UAW) union local at the McDonnell Douglas plant in Long Beach, California have begun to identify a range of civilian projects that could be produced at that plant. The Oil, Chemical and Atomic Workers union local at the DoE's Piketon, Ohio gaseous diffusion plant has begun a long-term "Atomic Reclamation and Conversion Project" to begin planning for new industrial possibilities to replace the declining nuclear weapons and nuclear power related role of that facility.

There are unique problems of re-adjustment for workers accustomed to the single customer, high performance, relatively high cost realm of military production. Even so, the general problem of finding employment for workers displaced by structural changes in the US economy has many points in common with the economic conversion problem. The International Association of Machinists, which has more workers in military industry than any other US union, has proposed a "Rebuilding America Act." The act covers conversion from military to civilian production along with problems of runaway shops and declining industries. The Machinists plan proposes two funding mechanisms—a Pension Fund Development Bank and loans from the existing Federal Financing Bank—capable of supporting alternative industrial production in response to local development plans where private capital is not forthcoming. By proposing funding mechanisms for alternative civilian production, the Machinists plan goes beyond existing conversion proposals.

Conclusion

The economic opportunities offered by a nuclear Freeze far outweigh its costs. A Freeze would potentially produce tens of billions of dollars of immediate budget savings. At its worst, a Freeze would displace 350,000 workers in military industry. If cutbacks in nuclear weapons system funding are matched by civilian government spending or a tax cut, overall employment could rise under a Freeze.

If Freeze budget savings were targeted toward particular problems—from income maintenance, nutrition, and education to cutting Federal budget deficits—they would provide a significant step towards solving pressing national economic problems. Arms control proposals cannot be expected to cure the nation's accumulated economic ills. Nonetheless, a Freeze does offer more economic opportunities than are generally associated with proposals to cut military spending.

No shift of resources as large as that entailed in stopping production of a whole new generation of nuclear weapons systems simultaneously can occur without problems. However, careful planning and a national approach to economic conversion can minimize these transition problems. Even in the absence of conversion planning, the disruptive economic effects of a halt in nuclear weapons production will be much less severe than many have assumed.

Ultimately, any serious and orderly approach to arms reductions must incorporate a strategy for minimizing the attendant economic disruption. CEP offers this study as another step in the necessary national debates about nuclear weapons policy and economic security. As long as large numbers of workers and communities view military spending as their most viable economic option, arms control proposals will have difficulty receiving the serious and active consideration they deserve. If this study clarifies the dimensions of this problem and stimulates further debate on how to solve it, it will have achieved its purpose.

Table I

States Receiving the Largest Prime Contract Awards for Missiles and Bombers Covered by a Freeze, FY 1982

($ MILLION)

	1 CA	2 WA	3 CO	4 FL	5 MA	6 OH	7 NY	8 MO	9 UT	10 MI	11 MD
B-1 Bomber	$1,293.3	--	--	--	--	$269.1	$198.5	--	--	--	--
Cruise	449.1	109.8	--	--	--	2.3	--	$224.6	--	$165.0	$ 89.1
Trident	896.7	--	--	$ 9.1	$155.8	--	43.3	--	--	--	16.3
Pershing	--	--	--	351.9	14.0	7.6	--	--	--	--	--
MX	685.2	77.0	$452.3	37.0	225.4	--	--	--	$179.6	--	--
TOTAL	$3,324.3	$466.3	$452.3	$398.0	$395.2	$279.0	$241.8	$224.6	$179.6	$165.0	$105.4
% Total National Prime Contracts $6,566.0	50.6%	7.1%	6.9%	6.1%	6.0%	4.2%	3.7%	3.4%	2.7%	2.5%	1.6%

Source: US Department of Defense, Washington Headquarters Services, Directorate of Information, Operations and Reports. "Alphabetic Detail of DoD Prime Contracts over $10,000, FY 1982."

115

Table II

Dependence of the Eight Largest Nuclear Contractors
on Nuclear Delivery Vehicle Contracts

Contractor	Total Nuclear Delivery Vehicle Awards ($ million)	Nuclear Awards as % DoD Awards	Nuclear Awards as % Total Sales[a]
Rockwell International	$1,644.5	61.1%	21.6%
B-1	1,299.9		
MX	344.6		
Boeing	$875.2	26.6%	9.7%
B-52[b]	488.4		
ALCM	95.9		
GLCM/SLCM	13.0		
B-1B	277.9		
Martin Marietta	$803.6	40.0%	22.8%
MX	452.3		
Pershing	351.3		
Lockheed			
Trident	$776.5	22.2%	13.8%
General Electric	$350.7	9.6%	1.3%
MX	50.4		
GLCM/SLCM	0.262		
B-1B	256.6		
Trident	43.4		
General Dynamics[c]			
GLCM/SLCM	$341.8	5.8%	5.5%
McDonnell Douglas			
GLCM/SLCM	$217.8	3.8%	2.9%
Northrop[d]			
MX	$214.0	13.3%	8.6%

Source: US Department of Defense, Washington Headquarters Services, Directorate of Information, Operations, and Reports, ''Alphabetic Detail of DoD Prime Contracts over $10,000, FY 1982.

Continued

a   Company fiscal years do not all coincide with the government fiscal years for which contract information is available, so the military contracts as a percentage of sales may not match figures in company annual report.

b   This represents all Boeing prime contract awards for work on B-52s in FY 1982. According to company reports cited in Investor Responsibility Research Center, *The Nuclear Weapons Industry* (Washington: IRRC 1984), the firm received $238 million in 1982 (calendar year) for fitting B-52s to carry ALCMs.

c   These figures do not include General Dynamics' awards for work on the Trident submarine.

d   Northrop award figures would be higher if information on awards for its classified "Stealth" bomber work were available.

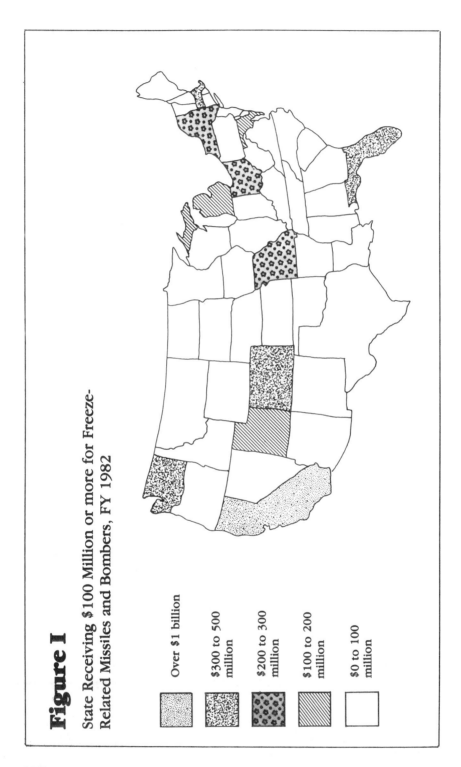

Figure I

State Receiving $100 Million or more for Freeze-Related Missiles and Bombers, FY 1982

Over $1 billion

$300 to 500 million

$200 to 300 million

$100 to 200 million

$0 to 100 million

Figure II

Employment per $1 Billion Spent, Guided Missile
Production and Other Selected Industries and Services

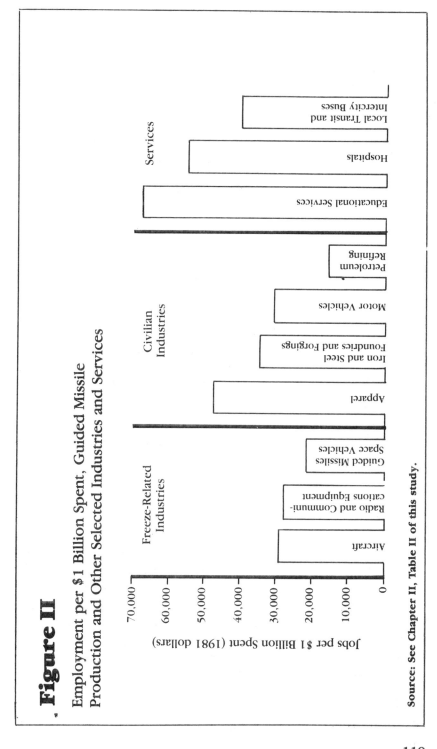

Source: See Chapter II, Table II of this study.

119

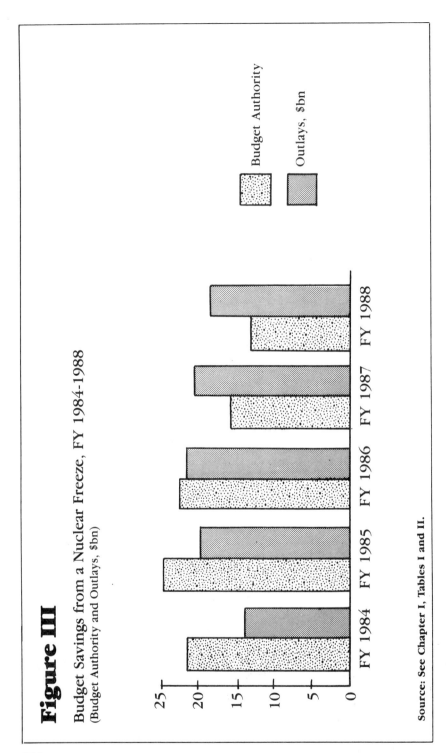

Figure III

Budget Savings from a Nuclear Freeze, FY 1984-1988
(Budget Authority and Outlays, $bn)

Budget Authority

Outlays, $bn

FY 1984   FY 1985   FY 1986   FY 1987   FY 1988

25
20
15
10
5
0

Source: See Chapter I, Tables I and II.

Council on Economic Priorities

You Can Make a Difference!

Join CEP Today!

☐ **Please enroll me as a Sustaining Member of CEP** and send me a copy of all CEP **Reports** and **Newsletters.** Membership $50. (Tax deductible.)

☐ **Please enroll me as a Regular Member of CEP** and send me a copy of all CEP **Newsletters.** Membership $25. Students, unemployed and retired persons $10. (Tax deductible.)

☐ Please send me information on Institutional and Public Library subscriptions.
212/691-8550

Name _____

Street_____Apt. _____

City _____

State_____ Zip _____

(All contributions are tax deductible.)

Council on Economic Priorities, 84 Fifth Ave., New York, NY 10011